Hitler and the Rise of the Nazi Party

Hitler and the Rise of the Nazi Party

2nd Edition

Frank McDonough

Routledge
Taylor & Francis Group

LONDON AND NEW YORK

First published 2003 by Pearson Education Limited
Second edition published 2012

Published 2014 by Routledge
2 Park Square, Milton Park, Abingdon, Oxon OX14 4RN
711 Third Avenue, New York, NY 10017, USA

Routledge is an imprint of the Taylor & Francis Group, an informa business

Copyright © 2012, Taylor & Francis.

The right of Frank McDonough to be identified as author of this work has been asserted
by him in accordance with the Copyright, Designs and Patents Act 1988.

ISBN 13: 978-1-4082-6921-3 (pbk)

British Library Cataloguing in Publication Data
A CIP record for this book can be obtained from the British Library

Library of Congress Cataloguing in Publication Data
McDonough, Frank, 1957-
    Hitler and the rise of the Nazi Party / Frank McDonough. -- Second edition.
        pages cm. -- (Seminar studies)
    Includes bibliographical references.
    ISBN 978-1-4082-6921-3 (pbk.)
    1. Hitler, Adolf, 1889-1945.   2. Nationalsozialistische Deutsche Arbeiter-Partei.
3. Germany--Politics and government--1918-1933.   4. Germany--Politics and
government--1933-1945.   I. Title.
    DD247.H5M357 2012
    324.243'0238--dc23
                                                                    2011049353

Set in 10/13.5pt Berkeley Book by 35

Introduction to the series

History is narrative constructed by historians from traces left by the past. Historical enquiry is often driven by contemporary issues and, in consequence, historical narratives are constantly reconsidered, reconstructed and reshaped. The fact that different historians have different perspectives on issues means that there is also often controversy and no universally agreed version of past events. *Seminar Studies* was designed to bridge the gap between current research and debate, and the broad, popular general surveys that often date rapidly.

The volumes in the series are written by historians who are not only familiar with the latest research and current debates concerning their topic, but who have themselves contributed to our understanding of the subject. The books are intended to provide the reader with a clear introduction to a major topic in history. They provide both a narrative of events and a critical analysis of contemporary interpretations. They include the kinds of tools generally omitted from specialist monographs: a chronology of events, a glossary of terms and brief biographies of 'who's who'. They also include bibliographic essays in order to guide students to the literature on various aspects of the subject. Students and teachers alike will find that the selection of documents will stimulate discussion and offer insight into the raw materials used by historians in their attempt to understand the past.

Clive Emsley and Gordon Martel
Series Editors

Contents

Publisher's acknowledgements

We are grateful to the following for permission to reproduce copyright material:

Text

Documents 2, 6, 10, 11, 15, 19 and 20 from *Nazism 1919–1945. Vol. 1: The Rise to Power*, University of Exeter Press (Noakes, J. and Pridham, G. 1983); Document 3 from the Avalon Project at Yale Law Library; Document 9 from *Mein Kampf*, Vol. 2, Paternoster (Hitler, A. 1938) pp. 525–36, Bavarian State Ministry of Finance; Document 18 from 'How do we struggle against a Third Reich?' in *The Weimar Republic Sourcebook* edited by Anton Kaes, Martin Jay, Edward Dimendberg. © 1994 by the Regents of the University of California. Reprinted by permission of the University of California Press.

Picture Credits

The publisher would like to thank the following for their kind permission to reproduce their photographs:

Plate 1 from Getty Images/Three Lions, Plate 2 from Getty Images/Daily Herald Archive, Plate 3 from Getty Images/Popperfoto and Plate 4 from Getty Images/Popperfoto.

Chronology

1918

11 November   Germany signs armistice to end First World War

1919

7 April   Bavarian Soviet republic proclaimed in Munich (later suppressed by right-wing forces)

28 June   Treaty of Versailles signed

September   Adolf Hitler joins the German Workers' Party

1920

24 February   Hitler announces new 25-point programme of the National Socialist German Workers Party (NSDAP)

1921

29 July   Adolf Hitler becomes undisputed leader of the Nazi Party

1922

18 July   'Law to protect the Republic' passed by the Reichstag

1923

11 January   French and Belgian troops occupy the Ruhr to enforce payment of reparations. German government offers a policy of 'passive resistance'

Summer   The 'great inflation' grips Germany, resulting in a complete collapse of the German Mark

26 September   Kahr declares state of emergency in Bavaria

27 September   President Ebert declares state of emergency throughout Germany

8 November   Munich Beer Hall Putsch

1924

1 April   Hitler sentenced to five years detention for 'high treason' (released in December 1924)

9 August   Dawes Plan on reparations payments announced

1925

28 February   President Ebert dies

27 April   Paul von Hindenburg, military figure from First World War, is elected as President

5 October   Locarno Treaty signed

1926

8 September   Germany joins the League of Nations

1927

31 January   The Allied military control mission is withdrawn from Germany

1928

20 May   In the Reichstag elections the Nazis poll a mere 2.8% of total votes cast

1929

3 October   Gustav Stresemann dies

29 October   Wall Street stock market crash

1930

30 March   Brüning appointed Chancellor

14 September   The Nazi Party makes a spectacular breakthrough in the Reichstag elections, polling 18% of votes, and holding 107 seats in the new parliament

1932

10 April   Hindenburg re-elected President in run-off election against Adolf Hitler who polls 13 million votes

13 April   Hitler's Stormtroopers (SA) banned

30 May   Brüning resigns as Chancellor and is replaced by Franz von Papen

17 June   Ban on the SA is lifted

31 July   In the Reichstag elections, the Nazi Party polls 37.3% of the total votes, holds 230 seats in the new parliament and is now the most popular party in Germany

6 November   In the second Reichstag elections of the year, the Nazi vote falls by 2 million and their seats in parliament fall to 196

17 November   Papen resigns as Chancellor

2 December   General von Schleicher is appointed Chancellor

1933

30 January   Adolf Hitler is appointed German Chancellor

Who's who

Amann, Max (1891–1957) was born in Munich and met Hitler during his service in the army in the First World War. In 1921, he became the business manager of the Nazi Party. In 1922 he was appointed as Director of the party publishing house (Eher Verlag), which published *Mein Kampf*. He played a leading role in the management of the party newspaper (*Völkischer Beobachter*). After the fall of the Third Reich, Amann attempted to portray himself as a businessman, with no real commitment towards Nazism. In 1948, he was sentenced to 10 years in a labour camp during the de-Nazification trials. He died in poverty in Munich in 1957.

Brüning, Heinrich (1885–1970) German Chancellor from 1930 to 1932 and leader of the Catholic Centre Party. He led Germany at the height of the depression. His deflationary policies proved extremely unpopular. He resigned in May 1932. In 1934, he fled to Switzerland and then went to live in the USA eventually becoming a Professor of Political Science at Harvard University. He died in the USA in 1970.

Drexler, Anton (1884–1942), a Munich locksmith, who founded the German Workers' Party (DAP) in 1919, which subsequently turned into the Nazi Party. He viewed the DAP as a classless, popular party, which espoused nationalism and was anti-capitalist, anti-Liberal and anti-Marxist. After Hitler took over the leadership of the Nazi Party, Drexler faded into the background and after 1924 never participated in the Nazi Party ever again. In February 1942, Drexler died a forgotten man.

Eckart, Dietrich (1868–1923). A poet, with a drinking problem. He was Hitler's first 'mentor', and was described by the Nazi leader as the 'spiritual' godfather of the movement. Eckart helped to obtain the funds to buy the Völkischer Beobachter, and he introduced Hitler to several leading figures in the Bavarian upper class. Hitler dedicated *Mein Kampf* to Eckart. It is believed Eckart greatly influenced Hitler's developing anti-Semitism. Eckart's health was made worse by his alcoholism and his addiction to morphine. He died in 1923.

Feder, Gottfried (1883–1941). He was known as the Nazi 'economic expert' during the early days of the party. Feder advocated the control of interest levied by banks. He helped to draft the 25-point Nazi Party programme. Yet Feder's anti-capitalist ideas were never adopted when the Nazi Party came to power, and he ceased to play a leading role in the party. He died in 1941 a forgotten figure.

Goebbels, Joseph (1897–1945). The master 'spin doctor' of the Nazi Party. He was unusual among the members of the early Nazi Party as he held a doctorate, an academic qualification, despised by most leading Nazis who saw war medals as the best qualification for membership of the party. He suffered from polio in his childhood and had a club foot, which tormented him, especially during the era of the Third Reich, as it meant he did not match up physically to the ideal member of a master race. He started out on the 'socialist' wing of the Nazi Party and only became a key member of Hitler's elite after 1926. His sharp intelligence, his brilliant skills at propaganda and his ideological passion for Nazism all served to make him a central figure in the Nazi Party, whose propaganda abilities were quite outstanding and greatly aided the rise of the party. Goebbels was a violent anti-Semite, and he remained a deeply committed Nazi right up until his suicide in Hitler's bunker in Berlin in April 1945. His wife also committed suicide with him after administering poison to all their six children.

Goering, Hermann (1893–1946). A leading figure in the Nazi Party and the second most powerful figure in the Third Reich. He was a highly decorated pilot during the First World War, and his prestige as a war hero made him a leading and much admired figure in the early Nazi Party. In 1923, he took part in the Munich Beer Hall Putsch and was seriously wounded. He played a leading role in Hitler's rise to power through his close relations with leading figures in the army. After Hitler came to power, Goering helped to create the Gestapo, the Nazi secret police and later became commander of the Luftwaffe. On 9 May 1945, Goering was captured by American forces and was put on trial at Nuremberg in 1946. Yet only two hours before his execution was to take place for 'war crimes', he took a capsule of cyanide, which he had hidden from his guards during his captivity.

Hess, Rudolf (1894–1987) A leading figure in the early Nazi Party and deputy leader of the Nazi Party. He took part in the Beer Hall Putsch and served his sentence in Landsberg fortress in 1923. From 1925 to 1932, he acted as Hitler's personal secretary. In May 1941, Hess flew to Britain on a 'peace mission', seemingly without the permission of Hitler, who declared him 'insane'. He was sentenced to life imprisonment at the Nuremberg trials and spent the rest of his life in Spandau prison, guarded by the Russians, who refused to release him.

Hindenburg, Paul von (1847–1934) President of Germany from 1925 to 1934 and the person who appointed Hitler as Chancellor in January 1933. He was a leading Prussian landowner and military figure, who was Field Marshal during the First World War. As President, he was supported by a coalition of nationalists, army commanders, aristocrats, conservatives and industrialists. After 1930, he used Article 48 of the constitution to appoint a series of right-wing figures who pushed Germany in an anti-democratic direction. After Hitler came to power, Hindenburg remained President until his death in August 1934.

Hitler, Adolf (1889–1945) The Leader of the Nazi Party, the Führer of the German people during the era of the Third Reich, and one of the most significant figures in history. He was born in Braunau am Inn, Austria on 20 April 1889. He left school at sixteen without qualifications and spent time in Vienna and Munich before enlisting for the German army in 1914. He joined the German Workers' Party in 1919, which soon turned into the Nazi Party. His brilliant speeches were what brought him and the Nazi Party to prominence in German politics. He developed during the 1920s into a shrewd politician, and eventually persuaded Hindenburg to bring him to power. He turned Germany into a personal dictatorship. He committed suicide in his Berlin bunker in April 1945 having left Europe and Germany totally devastated.

Hugenberg, Alfred (1865–1951), was a press and film tycoon who led the German National People's Party (DNVP) from 1928 to 1933. He was a strong nationalist who had been a co-founder of the Pan-German League. He helped Hitler achieve national recognition during the campaign by the right against the Young Plan. He wanted to build a right-wing alliance with Hitler, but the Nazi leader refused to tie himself to someone he thought of as an 'old bourgeois Conservative'. Even so, Hugenburg supported Hitler coming to power and the votes of the DNVP allowed the Nazis to pass the Enabling Act (1933), which paved the way for the creation of Nazi rule in Germany. After the war, Hugenberg was allowed to retain his property and business interests and he was not penalised by the de-Nazification courts. He died in 1951.

Ludendorff, Erich (1865–1937) was the virtual 'dictator' of Germany during the latter stages of the First World War. He played a prominent role in the Munich Beer Hall Putsch, even though he escaped prosecution. He ran for President in 1925, but received only 1.1% of the votes. Relations between Hitler and Ludendorff deteriorated in the late 1920s and even though he was never given a role in the Third Reich, he did receive a state funeral after his death in December 1937.

Papen, Franz von (1879–1969) was Chancellor of Germany in 1932 and played a leading role in helping Hitler gain power. After the Nazis came to power, Papen was made deputy Chancellor, but his influence over Hitler was minimal. In June 1934 he called for the Nazi leader to deal with 'extremists' in the Stormtroopers (SA). After the blood purge of the SA later the same month, Papen resigned, but he continued to loyally serve Hitler's regime. He was found not guilty of 'war crimes' at the Nuremberg trial in 1946, but was sentenced to eight years in a labour camp in a de-Nazification trial a year later. Released in 1949, he wrote his memoirs in the early 1950s and he died in 1969.

Röhm, Ernst (1887–1934) was the Chief of Staff of the Nazi Stormtroopers (SA) and a leading figure in the early history of the party. After the Nazis came to power Röhm expected the SA to be turned into a Nazi 'People's Army', but this idea was opposed by Hitler and the regular army. He was murdered in the blood purge, known as the 'Night of the Long Knives' in June 1934.

Rosenberg, Alfred (1893–1946) was the self-styled 'philosopher' of the early Nazi Party. He was a strong proponent of the idea that the Nazis had to create a 'master race' while in power or else Germany would cease to be a major force in the world. In 1934, he was given the grand title of 'The Führer's Delegate for the entire intellectual and Philosophical Education and Instruction of the National Socialist Party'. During the war, Rosenberg did play a key part in seizing Jewish property in occupied territories. In June 1941, he was appointed Minister of the occupied eastern territories and was heavily involved in the implementation of the 'Final Solution' of the Jewish question. He was found guilty and hanged in October 1946, after being sentenced to death at the Nuremberg trials.

Schleicher, Kurt von (1882–1934) was the last German Chancellor of the Weimar Republic, but was only in power for fifty-seven days. He wanted to institute a military dictatorship, but Hindenburg refused, and he was dismissed from office on 28 January 1933. Hitler never forgave him for attempting to prevent him from gaining power, and he was killed by Nazis in June 1934 during the 'Night of the Long Knives'.

Strasser, Gregor (1892–1934) was the leading figure in the north German wing of the Nazi Party before 1933. He supported many 'socialist' ideas such as bringing industry and land under state control and curbing the powers of banks, and big business. He wanted the Nazi Party to gain support from the working classes and because of this, he increasingly came into conflict with Hitler, as the party moved towards attracting the middle class and business groups in the early 1930s. He resigned from the party in December 1932 and left politics. On 30 June 1934, he was murdered during the 'Night of the Long Knives'.

Strasser, Otto (1897–1974), the younger brother of Gregor Strasser. He was a leading 'socialist' radical in the northern wing of the Nazi Party before 1933. His support for the 'socialist' parts of the programme brought him to a collision course with Hitler. After refusing to accept the Nazi Party was anti-capitalist, he was expelled from the party in July 1930. After Hitler came to power, he went into exile abroad. He died in Munich in August 1974.

Glossary of terms and organisations

Deutsche Arbeiterpartei (DAP): The German Workers' Party, founded by Anton Drexler, a Munich locksmith. It was this party which Hitler joined and which later became the Nazi Party.

Deutsch-Nationale Volkspartei (DNVP): The German National People's Party, the leading conservative party in Weimar Germany. This party moved to the extreme right during the early 1930s and was keen to ally with the Nazis: something which Hitler resisted. The DNVP voted for the Enabling Act in 1933 which set up Hitler's dictatorship.

Freikorps: Free Corps: The paramilitary units composed of ex-soldiers that sprang up throughout Germany after 1918. This group of former soldiers helped the nationalist right to deal with the communist threat in the immediate aftermath of the First World War.

Führer: Leader (Adolf Hitler). Hitler was the undisputed leader of the Nazi Party and enjoyed total power over the decision making within the Nazi Party.

Gau: District.

Gauleiter: District leader of the Nazi Party. A very powerful figure within local Nazi parties. As Hitler appointed each *Gauleiter*, he was able to exert important influence over local parties. After 1933, the *Gauleiter* system was added to the local government system in Nazi Germany.

Herrenvolk: Master race. The term was reserved for the supposed future 'racial elite' that would rule the Third Reich.

Hitler-Jugend: Hitler Youth. This organisation became a very important means of bringing young people into the Nazi Party. After 1933, the Hitler Youth became a key Nazi youth movement, which every young German was required to join.

KPD: The German Communist Party. The German Communist Party took its ideas from Marx, but its orders from the leaders of the Soviet Union. The Party refused to co-operate with the SPD, branding its members 'social fascists'. Many of its leaders thought that if Hitler was given power his incompetence could herald the end of the capitalist system in Germany and pave the way for the outbreak of a communist revolution.

Landstag: The legislature of each German regional state.

Lebensraum: Living space. A key concept in Hitler's foreign policy thinking. The idea was for the German armed forces not only to defeat the enemy but also to de-populate areas captured and use them to expand Germans on to the newly acquired land.

Mittelstand: Middle class. The middle class, usually the backbone of an effective democracy, suffered severe economic trauma during the 'great inflation of 1923' and after the 1929 Wall Street Crash. The middle class were always over-represented among Nazi members and voters, prompting one writer to describe Nazism as a 'revolt from the middle'.

Nationalsozialistische Deutsche Arbeiterpartei (NSDAP): The National Socialist German Workers Party, the full title of the Nazi Party. The party grew rapidly in support from 1928 onwards to become the most popular political party in Germany at the time when Hitler came to power.

ReichsFührer-SS: Leader of the SS (position occupied by Heinrich Himmler from 1929 to 1945). Himmler's racial anti-Semitism was to play a much more prominent role in the era of the Third Reich than in the period before 1933 when the SS was an elite security force whose principal aim was to protect Hitler at Nazi meetings.

Reichskanzler: Reich Chancellor.

Reichstag: German parliament. The Reichstag became increasingly powerless to save democracy, largely because of the increased use of Article 48 of the Weimar Constitution, which allowed the President to bypass parliamentary rule as and when he thought there was an 'emergency'.

Reichswehr: The name of the Defensive Land Army created under the Weimar Republic. (In 1935, it was renamed the Wehrmacht.) The army played a very shady role during the Weimar period and was keen to support Hitler's rise to power, as many Generals were anti-communist and saw the Nazis as allies in dealing with the communist threat and likely to support increased spending on the armed forces.

Sturmabteilungen (SA): The Stormtroopers or 'Brownshirts', founded in 1921 as the private army of the Nazi Party, led by Ernst Röhm. Hitler viewed the

SA as useful bully boys, but he did not feel they were an integral part of his racial elite and he refused to support the idea the SA would play a leading role within the armed forces of the Third Reich.

Sozialdemokratische Partei Deutschlands (SPD): The Social Democratic Party. The SPD was the biggest supporter of Weimar democracy, but after 1928, it ceased to be involved in government, lost support from voters and was ultimately powerless to prevent the collapse of democracy.

Schutzstaffel-SS: Hitler's black-shirted personal bodyguard, which grew into the most powerful Nazi organisation during the era of the Third Reich.

Stahlhelm: Steel Helmet: A leading Nationalist ex-soldiers organisation, which operated during the Weimar era.

Volk: Race. A central concept in Nazi ideology. Indeed, recent studies are showing just how integral racial ideas were within the Nazi elite.

Volkisch: Racial: ethnic: nationalist.

Völkischer Beobachter: Racial Observer: The Official Nazi Party newspaper. It is now known that army secret funds helped to finance the purchase of this newspaper.

Volksdeutsche: Ethnic Germans.

Volksgemeinschaft: The Folk Community. The Nazi slogan expressing the desire to create a classless unified German society.

Zentrum: The Catholic Centre Party.

Part 1

BACKGROUND

1

The Vulnerabilities of Weimar Democracy, 1918–1933

INTRODUCTION

On 30 January 1933, Adolf Hitler was appointed Chancellor of Germany by President Paul von Hindenburg. Hitler was placed in the position to lead Germany by a truly remarkable surge of popular support in democratic elections. In July 1932, the Nazi Party became the nation's largest political party, supported by 13.7 million voters representing 37.2 per cent of the electorate. Hitler made no secret of his bitter hatred of parliamentary democracy, vowed to sweep it away, crush communism, remove Jews from society and embark on a vast programme of rearmament. It was clear such policies could only be achieved through a one-party dictatorship. By 1945 Hitler's regime had led directly and indirectly to the deaths of 55 million people in the Second World War. No other comparable example of such a destructive, violent and inhumane regime coming to power by democratic and constitutional means exists.

There is a very familiar interpretation of the rise of Hitler to power, which is constantly repeated in many studies of the subject. It suggests the Weimar Republic was deeply unpopular and associated with: the fall of the Kaiser; the crushing burden of the Versailles Treaty; and the trauma of the 'great inflation'. It only survived between 1918 and 1923 with the help of the army. Between 1924 and 1928 US loans gave a fragile mirage of economic stability. This was shattered after the 1929 Wall Street Crash which cut off vital loans and led to an unprecedented economic collapse, mass unemployment and deep political instability. Between 1930 and 1933 Hindenburg dispensed with parliamentary coalitions and ruled arbitrarily instead using Article 48 of the constitution, which gave him unlimited 'emergency powers'. In the same period, Nazi support grew spectacularly on the extreme right, while support for the communists rose markedly on the extreme left leading to unprecedented street violence. By 1933, after trying out Heinrich Brüning, Franz von

Papen and General Kurt von Schleicher, as German Chancellors – all of whom were deeply unpopular, Hindenburg was finally and reluctantly persuaded to appoint Hitler Chancellor at the head of a 'National Coalition' – containing only three Nazis. He hoped the Conservative right could manipulate and control Hitler to do its bidding. As Alan Bullock put it: 'Hitler was jobbed into office by the old reactionary conservative old guard precisely at a time when his electoral popularity had peaked.' This interpretation places strong emphasis on the weaknesses of the Weimar democratic system that became subverted to serve the needs of reactionary forces of the right. The old conservative right – so this argument continues – could have gone on ignoring Hitler's claim to power and found an alternative leader. Detlev Peukert has argued Hitler's appeal to those who brought him in to office lay in the fact he promised a 'return to the past' using the power of a modern state. If we accept this interpretation Hitler's rise to power was a monumental political miscalculation made possible by a flawed political system.

It would be wrong to completely dismiss this long-standing explanation completely, but it is deeply flawed. One pressing question it ignores is: why did over 13 million people, of their own free will, support Hitler and the Nazi Party? Something clearly monumental was going on in Germany after 1929 that changed the psychology of voters in a seismic fashion. No democratic party has ever risen from such relative obscurity to such mass support in so short a period of time. It was not economic misfortune alone that explains this upsurge in Nazi voters. The unemployed, who were most deeply affected by the 'Great Depression', still voted predominantly for the parties of the left – the **SPD** and the communist **KPD**.

So Hitler's deeply emotional appeal to regenerate Germany clearly struck a chord with millions of voters. Hitler was not so much jobbed into office, as blown into office by a wind of change, affecting a very large portion of German society. The rise of Hitler and Nazism was not – as we shall see – the inevitable consequence of a flawed political system, brought to its knees by economic problems, but rather a unique revolution, with a genuine appeal to millions of voters. Hitler promised a new collective national identity, which would bring a return to stability, restore optimism and provide a forward-looking momentum. Millions of Germans saw Hitler's promise as the best way out of a crisis that democracy seemed incapable of solving. Hitler's appeal, therefore, embodied a strong desire to bring order out of chaos by establishing a united, patriotic and supposedly classless 'National Community'. Nazi propaganda spread this message – by creating the image of Hitler as a strong leader and giving the Nazi Party a clear brand identity through the use of mass rallies, torchlight parades, flags, posters, and symbols. Above all, the Nazis offered supporters a chance of deep personal and emotional belonging to a 'Movement'.

Sozialdemokratische Partei Deutschlands (SPD): The Social Democratic Party. The SPD was the biggest supporter of Weimar democracy, but after 1928, it ceased to be involved in government, lost support from voters and was ultimately powerless to prevent the collapse of democracy.

KPD: The German Communist Party. The German Communist Party took its ideas from Marx, but its orders from the leaders of the Soviet Union. The Party refused to cooperate with the SPD, branding its members 'social fascists'. Many of its leaders thought that if Hitler was given power his incompetence could herald the end of the capitalist system in Germany and pave the way for the outbreak of a communist revolution.

So the real answer as to why Hitler came to power lies in the personality and ideology of Adolf Hitler; in the sources left behind by those who decided to support the Nazi Party; through close analysis of the voting patterns of Nazi voters in the crucial period after 1930 when Nazi support surged; the way Hitler as a clever and instinctive politician profited from chronic economic problems and the miscalculations of his opponents; and finally by examining the fatal miscalculations and clandestine intrigues surrounding the ageing President Hindenburg, who was finally persuaded by his close advisers to appoint the Nazi leader as Chancellor. Yet it was the German voters who voted for Hitler in the first place who had placed Hitler in the prime position to lead Germany to disaster.

THE IMPACT OF WAR

In Germany, there had been enthusiasm bordering on hysteria when the First World War began in August 1914. Germans were supremely confident that their armed force would triumph in the struggle for mastery of Europe. The army high command had planned – as was the Prussian way of war – a rapid war of movement. But after the initial Battle of the Marne, the conflict lapsed into a long war of attrition, in the trenches of the western front. Even so, the German army of 1914–1918 was unquestionably the most fearsome fighting unit yet assembled. In 1917, the war on the eastern front ended in a German victory. Not even Napoleon or Hitler could match that. In 1918, the Germans came close to a decisive breakthrough on the western front via the Ludendorff offensive, but the western Allies attritional tactics, enriched by thousands of fresh US troops and a crippling naval blockade finally gave them the edge. By the autumn of 1918, the German army was completely worn out and in disarray. The unthinkable was about to happen. Germany was about to lose the First World War, without enemy troops ever setting foot on German soil. This was shocking and incomprehensible. The returning soldiers felt they had not been defeated in battle by superior military opponents, but rather, 'stabbed in the back' by 'liberals', 'socialists', and 'Jewish profiteers' on the Home Front. These soldiers never realised the entire war effort had been financed by vast government borrowing that was supposed to be repaid by Germany's defeated opponents. Instead, the losing power now had to pay. The psychological trauma of defeat in the First World War had profound military, political and economic consequences.

Once it became apparent that the final German offensive had failed, Erich Ludendorff and Paul von Hindenburg, the two leading army commanders, recommended a new government be formed, with the primary aim of broker-ing an armistice. This was a cynical ploy designed to deflect blame for the defeat away from the Kaiser's regime and the army on to a newly formed democratic government. The Generals thought a democratic administration – which the Allies were demanding anyway – might ward off a communist revolution and broker favourable peace terms. The Armistice came into effect on 11 November 1918. All German troops were forced to withdraw east of the Rhine, the punitive Treaty of Brest-Litovsk, which Germany imposed on the Soviet Union, was declared null and void. The German fleet was to surrender to the Allies, but this was avoided when naval chiefs scuttled their own vessels. This act of defiance was a portent of things to come. Kaiser Wilhelm, the German monarch, claimed – like most soldiers – that the German armed forces had been 'stabbed in the back' by what he called a 'secret, planned campaign of opponents at home' (Evans, 2003: 61).

THE GERMAN REVOLUTION OF 1918

The democratic Weimar Republic was thus born in the smouldering ashes of Germany's catastrophic military defeat. A 'revolution' soon swept the old regime from power in November 1918. Prince Max of Baden was appointed interim Chancellor, but all he did was announce that the Kaiser had abdicated and promptly resigned on 9 November at a time when Berlin was paralysed by a general strike. Here ended the 'Second Reich' established by Bismarck in 1871. The Hohenzollern dynasty, which had ruled Prussia for centuries, was also consigned to history. Friedrich Ebert, the leader of the Social Democrats, was now appointed the Chancellor of the new democratic German Republic – but the German 'revolution' was not over yet. A fight now raged within the parties on the left over who would lead the 'new' Germany. The three parties that vied for power were the Social Democratic Party (SPD) – a democratic socialist party, made up mostly of trade unionists; the Marxist-orientated Independent Socialists (USDP); and an even more extreme communist grouping called 'The Spartacists' – who later coalesced with other left-wing groups to form the Communist Party (KPD).

In December 1918, the USDP withdrew from the coalition 'provisional government' and the 'Spartacists' demanded a 'Soviet'-style communist revolution. Many communist councils had already established themselves in big cities, most notably in Munich, the capital of Bavaria. In January 1919, the SPD government brutally suppressed a left-wing Spartacist revolt, with the support of the German army and the **Free Corps**, a 400,000 strong group of trigger happy ex-soldiers incapable of fitting back into civilian society, who could be relied on to support the army in any counter-revolutionary conflict. Two leading communist figures, Karl Liebknecht and Rosa Luxemburg, were murdered by Free Corps officers on 15 January 1918. Only with the assistance

Freikorps: Free Corps: The paramilitary units composed of ex-soldiers that sprang up throughout Germany after 1918. This group of former soldiers helped the nationalist right to deal with the communist threat in the immediate aftermath of the First World War.

of the army and the Free Corps was communist revolution avoided. The consequences of this battle on the left of German politics was deeply significant. The SPD and the communists now became sworn enemies of each other and would no longer co-operate in any way whatsoever. The communists labelled Ebert and the SPD as 'social fascists'. The next threat to Weimar's fragile democracy was an attempted coup by renegade elements in the Germany army in March 1920, led by Dr Wolfgang Kapp (the 'Kapp Putsch'). This was supported by the Free Corps. The aim was to set up a right-wing military dictatorship that would restore the monarchy. In the early stages, leaders of the army refused to intervene to aid the democratic government. Only after a general strike, organised by the trade unions, did the army consent to put down the revolt and arrest the conspirators. Twice in the first eighteen months, democratic politicians needed the assistance of the army to save democracy.

THE IMPACT OF VERSAILLES

The terms of the Versailles Treaty, which were made public on 7 May 1919, dealt the new democratic German government another staggering economic and psychological blow. Angry protests took place throughout the country. Versailles was viewed on all sides as a vindictive treaty, designed to reduce Germany to a third-rate power. Germany had been defeated, but this seemed like international humiliation. Ebert described the terms as 'unrealisable and unbearable', but the agreement was signed on 28 June 1919 (Shirer, 1961: 81). Germany lost 13 per cent of its territory. The Rhineland was made a de-militarised zone and occupied. Alsace Lorraine returned to France. The newly created Polish state incorporated much of West Prussia and Upper Silesia within its borders. Danzig became a 'free city' under the nominal control of the newly created League of Nations. In order to give Poland access to the sea – a 'corridor' of land which separated East Prussia from the rest of Germany was created. All overseas colonies under German rule were redistributed under mandates issued by the League. Union between Austria and Germany was strictly forbidden. Other German-speaking minorities in central Europe were incorporated into Hungary, Yugoslavia and Czechoslovakia. Under punitive military clauses, the German army was reduced to just 100,000 and conscription banned. Naval staff were slimmed down to 15,000. Germany was prohibited from having battleships, destroyers, tanks, aircraft, heavy artillery guns and submarines. Germany now ranked as a military power alongside Greece and Argentina. Under Article 231 Germany was apportioned sole 'guilt' for starting the war. Finally, and even more controversially, Germany was obligated to pay financial compensation (reparations). The payments were supposed to continue in yearly instalments until 1983. An immediate down payment of five billion marks in gold was to be deposited between 1919 and 1921, along with deliveries of coal, cattle, ships and other goods to be paid in lieu of later cash payments. Any German government forced to sign such a treaty would have been deeply unpopular, so it was extremely unfortunate this grim task fell to the incoming SPD coalition government. It was like the owner of a new house being told on the first day of ownership that the roof had caved in and all the windows smashed. The tag of 'November criminals' hung around the necks of those democratic politicians who instigated the fall of the Kaiser and then signed the hated Versailles Treaty. It was a tag they never really shook off.

THE CULTURE OF VIOLENCE

Not surprisingly, the announcement of the Versailles terms led to a surge of support for right-wing nationalism and a period of deep political and economic unrest between 1918 and 1923. A powerful role here was played by soldiers returning from the war – the so-called 'Front Generation'. The bonds these men had forged in the self-sacrificing climate of the trenches survived the war. Most subscribed to the 'stab in the back myth', and resented the growth of socialism, democracy and communism that accompanied the 1918 revolution. This antagonism by the right towards the left was not new. During the era of the Anti-Socialist Law (1878–1890) there was government harassment, deportation and imprisonment of left-wing agitators and strike bans. But violence never went beyond limited street fighting. What happened in the Weimar era was very different. Ex-soldiers joined numerous paramilitary groups who confronted communists in street battles that led to hundreds of deaths and serious woundings. Several socialist politicians were also attacked or assassinated by right-wing extremists. Former SPD Chancellor Philipp Scheidemann had prussic acid thrown in his face in 1921, and Walter Rathenau, the Foreign Minister, was assassinated in 1922 en route to his office. There were more than 350 politically motivated murders by right-wing extremists during the Weimar era. Right-wing assassins often fled, sometimes aided by the police. When apprehended they were given ridiculously light sentences by anti-Republican judges. To put it bluntly, killing rather than just arguing with political opponents became part of the political culture of Weimar society.

Ex-soldiers roaming around the streets dressed up in various militaristic uniforms became another worrying feature of street life in the Weimar Republic. The most numerically strong of these Veterans Associations was the 'Steel Helmets League of Front Line Soldiers', founded on 13 November 1918 by Franz Seldte, the owner of a soda water factory in Magdeburg. By the mid-1920s it had 300,000 members and could offer a violent and intimidating militaristic presence on the streets. The manifesto of this group included a familiar litany of right-wing demands: destruction of the Versailles Treaty, the gaining of new 'living space', the restoration of the national flag of the Second Reich and the need for a 'strong patriotic leader'. In 1927, during a period when the Nazi Party was still a fringe party, and when there was a fragile economic recovery underway, 132,000 members of the Steel Helmets, dressed in military uniforms, organised a massive march past in Berlin as a demonstration of their continuing loyalty to the moribund 'Second Reich' of Kaiser Wilhelm, who was, by now, living in exile in Switzerland. Interestingly, the Steel Helmets, like many other Combat Leagues, and the Nazi Party, banned Jews from membership. To counteract these right-wing leagues, the Social Democrats set up their own uniformed group called 'The Reichsbanner' whose members pledged allegiance to the new democratic Republic. The Communists too established the 'Red Front Fighters' League' whose members increasingly confronted the Steel Helmets, the Free Corps and the Nazi Party's own violent uniformed paramilitary wing, the Stormtroopers (SA), in numerous demonstrations. It is very important to emphasise that violence in Germany did not start with Hitler and the Nazis. They magnified something that had become an integral part of Weimar political culture. The Nazis went on to integrate violence into the law and order organisations of the German state.

THE CONSTITUTION AND THE EMERGENCY POWERS OF THE PRESIDENT

The Constitution of the Weimar Republic, drafted by a special committee under the jurist Hugo Peuss and ratified in the spa town of Weimar on 31 July 1931, has been cited in almost every study of the rise of Hitler as the most important factor which made democracy inherently unstable. Germany had been a Federal state ever since 1871. This structure remained intact during the Weimar era. Central government controlled finance and foreign affairs, but a series of regional devolved state governments, known as Länder, had free rein to enact law regionally. Prussia – a Protestant region – was the most dominant German state, covering nearly 57 per cent of the German population. The second largest area was Bavaria – a Catholic area in the south – and the 'birthplace of the Nazi Party'.

National power resided in the German parliament, based in Berlin – which retained the title of '**Reichstag**'. All Germans – male and female – over the age of twenty could vote in elections at national and local level. The voting system was based on the exact proportional representation of the overall votes cast for each party in elections. For example, if a party received 30 per

Reichstag: German parliament. The Reichstag became increasingly powerless to save democracy, largely because of the increased use of Article 48 of the Weimar Constitution, which allowed the President to bypass parliamentary rule as and when he thought there was an 'emergency'.

cent of the votes it was allotted 30 per cent of seats in the Reichstag. A small fringe party could gain a seat if polling just 1 per cent of the poll. Yet the importance of fringe parties in affecting policy has been greatly exaggerated in many general studies of Weimar Germany. These small parties never gained more than 15 per cent of the overall votes in any election. They were never a reliable voting bloc at all, but little more than a ragbag of individualists and assorted right-wing eccentrics.

If a first-past-the-post system had operated – as in Britain – then a smaller number of parties would have ruled and maybe a more stable coalition government might have been formed, perhaps involving just two parties. Yet the Nazi Party might still have gained power under a first-past-the-post system and perhaps an overall majority when their support surged in the July 1932 National Elections. Proportional representation does not encourage political anarchy or facilitate a right-wing dictatorship. Such a system has worked well to produce compromise, co-operation and stable government in many countries, most notably, in post-war Germany. In Weimar Germany, however, coalition government led to frequent changes of government, and an overheated political atmosphere – a sort of perpetual election campaign – that undoubtedly diminished the respect and standing of democracy among the general population. Between 1919 and 1933 there were no fewer than twenty different Cabinets, each lasting an average of only eight months. The longest serving coalition was led by Hermann Muller between 1928 and 1930. Democracy looked like a system that provided no long-term stability. Germany's democratic politicians seemed very professional, but were mostly ageing and dull bureaucrats. No strong charismatic leader emerged in any of the traditional democratic political parties. This leadership vacuum gave Hitler a great advantage when the Nazi Party rose after 1928. Here was a man of action facing a group of dull faceless bureaucrats.

The only completely new aspect of the Weimar constitution was the creation of the post of President, elected by popular vote, as the new head of state. The post was designed to be an honorary figurehead role. The combination of a President, as head of state, with a democratically elected parliament was already firmly established in two stable democracies – France and the USA. We must keep this in mind when evaluating whether the seemingly flawed Weimar constitution should take all the blame for Hitler coming to power. The people who ran this system were far more important than the structure itself. No one realised how this democratic constitution could be subverted or manipulated. The President, elected every seven years, was given the subsidiary power under Article 48 of the constitution to appoint and dismiss elected governments and suspend civil rights at a time he alone judged to be a 'national emergency'. This was only designed for very 'exceptional circumstances'. It is often routinely suggested that President

Paul von Hindenburg abused this rule most flagrantly between 1925 and 1933. Yet Friedrich Ebert, the leader of the democratic SPD, who was President between 1918 until 1925 used Article 48 on a staggering 136 different occasions. He deposed democratically elected governments in Saxony and Thuringia to restore order. In 1920, during a civil war in the Ruhr, he issued a back-dated decree to impose death sentences on those who had participated in civil unrest. What this shows is that there were really no effective safeguards against the abuse of Article 48 and this did constitute a real threat to the survival of democracy, especially during a crisis period defined by the President as a 'national emergency'.

Ebert, who suffered from diabetes, died of a ruptured appendix on 18 February 1925, aged just 54. The Presidential election that followed proved a disaster for democracy. The right-wing persuaded Field Marshal Paul von Hindenburg, a key figure in Germany's militaristic armed forces during First World War, to stand. A victory for Hindenburg was a defeat for democracy and a first step, many thought, to a return of the Kaiser. Hindenburg won by a landslide in 1925. There is actually a very close correlation between those who voted for Hindenburg in 1925 and those who voted for the Nazi Party in the July 1932 election. Hindenburg was already a very old man when he came to power. Between 1925 and 1930 Hindenburg never used Article 48 a single time. It was only during the early 1930s when he came under the pernicious influence of a small inner circle of advisers, who were essentially militaristic and authoritarian in outlook, that Hindenburg used Article 48 to create governments of his own choosing. Hindenburg had little faith in democracy. He wanted to avoid making Hitler Chancellor, if it was practically possible, but he was guided – as we shall see later – by his advisers towards the idea of giving Hitler power. Hindenburg's historical reputation has been riddled as a consequence of making a decision he had desperately tried to avoid.

THE POLITICAL PARTIES

The large number of political parties in the Weimar period added yet another source of instability. In July 1932, for example, 27 different parties contested the national election and 15 won seats. The Liberals were divided between the German Democratic Party (DDP) and the more right-leaning German People's Party (DVP). Both these parties drew support from the fragmented middle classes. Their leaders saw themselves as capable of working constructively with Social Democrats to enact social welfare reforms. The Catholic Centre Party (**Zentrum**) remained more or less unchanged after 1918, though its Bavarian wing formed the Bavarian People's Party. It tended

Zentrum: The Catholic Centre Party.

to be strongest in rural communities in which there were strong traditional Catholic voters. The SPD, the DDP, the DVP and Zentrum were the parties most closely associated with the new political system. Most of the Weimar Chancellors came from the Centre Party or the National Liberal parties. The Centre Party polled around 5 million voters and gained on average 85 seats in the Reichstag. It was the only political party whose share of the vote never fluctuated during the Weimar era. The National Liberals were increasingly squeezed by left- and right-wing parties and their seats ranged from 75 to 40 in the early 1930s.

The SPD only filled the post of Reich Chancellor in four governments between 1919 and 1933. The SPD – as the representatives of the numerically large working class – stood the best chance of becoming Weimar's popular 'People's Party', but they lacked a popular leader, failed to unite the left and had precious little support from the middle classes. The SPD share of the vote in National elections went from a peak of 38 per cent in 1919 to 25 per cent in the election of 1932, which equated to around 160 seats. The SPD was superseded in July 1932 by the Nazi Party as Germany's most popular party, which emphasises the shift to the right that took place during the course of the Weimar Republic. The reluctance of the SPD to join coalitions made it seem like a party that preferred the luxury of opposition to the responsibilities of government. From 1923 to 1928 the SPD stayed outside national coalitions altogether. The last one in which the SPD participated was the Cabinet Müller – the so-called 'Grand Coalition' – between 1928 and 1930. Left of the SDP were the Independent Socialists (USD) and the much larger Communist Party (KPD), which gained the support of four and a half million voters in September 1930, and held 77 seats. The KPD – a pro-Stalinist Party – never deviated from their hatred of the SPD.

The parties on the conservative right demand close attention, as had they been more effective, support for the Nazi Party would not have grown so spectacularly. One in every three Nazi voters defected from the conservative parties. The leading right-wing conservative party was the **German National People's Party (DNVP)** formed through an amalgamation of the old pre-1914 Conservative Party, supported by other similar groups and special interest parties. Between 1919 and 1928 this party gained about 20 per cent of votes and reached a peak with 103 seats in December 1924, making it the second most popular party behind the SPD before 1930. The DNVP encompassed reactionary pro-Kaiser, Prussian militarists – elitists masquerading as popular politicians (dubbed 'Nazis in pin-striped suits') – who had no real sympathy with the masses and a 'Christian Social' wing that favoured limited welfare reforms. The DNVP supported the capitalist system, the army and the upholding of the landed interest. Beyond the DNVP were a bewildering number of small right-wing fringe and special interest parties. The Conservative right

Deutsch-Nationale Volkspartei (DNVP): The German National People's Party, the leading conservative party in Weimar Germany. This party moved to the extreme right during the early 1930s and was keen to ally with the Nazis: something which Hitler resisted. The DNVP voted for the Enabling Act in 1933 which set up Hitler's dictatorship.

– outside of the Nazi Party – discussed the need to create a new patriotic 'National Community'. Some on the traditional right drew inspiration from a popular book called 'The Third Reich', by a right-wing conservative called Arthur Moeller van den Bruck, which was published in 1922. This called for a 'new conservative revolution', under an authoritarian leader, who would create a 'National Community' which would unite all the classes in a Third Reich that would last for a thousand years. Even before the depression, a third of middle-class voters had abandoned the mainstream political parties altogether. There was a further substantial group of voters in small rural villages and towns who were alienated from the political system altogether. The right of German politics provided fertile ground for a radical and popular right-wing political party to exploit.

THE ANTI-DEMOCRATIC FORCES WITHIN THE GERMAN STATE

This deeply unstable politically diffuse political environment might have been compensated for by the support of the judiciary and the army for democracy. Yet the judges of Weimar, drawn from the old Conservative upper class, were anti-democratic in outlook almost without exception. They punished the communist left harshly, but offered lenient sentences for the crimes and street violence of right-wing Nationalist extremists. After the 'Kapp Putsch' in 1920 the government charged 705 people with 'high treason' but only one, the police chief in Berlin, received a prison sentence. In comparison, hundreds of socialists received punitive sentences for engaging in anti-government demonstrations. The leading army officers were also drawn from the upper echelons of German society. As we have seen, the army saved democracy from the twin threats of the extreme right and the left in the early years of Weimar, but it remained a law unto itself and was more preoccupied with shaking off the military restrictions placed upon it by the Versailles Treaty than upholding democracy. Repeated involvement of army officers in intrigues and plots designed to bring about authoritarian rule boded ill for the survival of democracy. Many leading army officers longed for a return of pre-1914 authoritarian military rule. The army could be relied upon to crush left-wing revolt, but was reluctant to deal with right-wing street violence. The army could have been subordinated to the Cabinet and Parliament, but it never was. Operating as a state within a state, the army was able to maintain its total independence of national government. In 1932 the army produced a secret report for President Hindenburg in which it advised that it could protect the Reich from communist violence and Nazi violence separately, but could not deal with both factions in the event of a civil war. The clear implication was that one of these groups needed to be suppressed and the army – like the Nazis – favoured cracking down on the communists.

ECONOMIC DIFFICULTIES

Another fact of life in Weimar Germany was constant economic difficulty. Germany was in a chronic state of economic recession between 1918 and 1924 and once again between 1929 and 1933. In 1923, a loaf of bread cost a wheelbarrow full of marks. The 'great inflation' was blamed on the Allies' attempt to obtain reparations payments, especially during the Franco-Belgian occupation of the Ruhr between 1923 and 1924. In order to prevent a complete economic meltdown, a new currency, the rentenmark, was introduced and loans from the USA via the Dawes Plan (1924) and the Young Plan (1929) allowed reparations to be paid with borrowed money. The 'great inflation' was a deeply traumatic episode, especially for the middle classes who saw their savings wiped out. In the period 1924–1929, known as the 'golden years' of Weimar, the German economy underwent a recovery, primarily due to loans from the USA. Wages rose to pre-war levels and new roads, schools and hospitals were built. Yet the extent of recovery was sluggish. Even in 1928, unemployment stood at 1.8 million.

In October 1929, when the US stock market collapsed, the German economy went into a meltdown. Of all the major European powers, Germany was most badly hit by the 'Great Depression', with unemployment soaring to a staggering six million of insured workers by 1932, but affecting up to 20 million people. Industrial production fell by 42 per cent. Agricultural prices fell dramatically and starvation was rife in rural areas. There is little doubt the economic collapse that occurred in Germany after 1929 intensified feelings against the Weimar Republic more sharply than ever before. Many Germans were looking for some way out of what seemed never-ending misery and perpetual crisis. Patience with democracy was running out. One party leader claimed to have the solution to all Germany's mounting problems. His name was Adolf Hitler.

Part 2

ANALYSIS

2

Adolf Hitler: Personality and Early Life

A dolf Hitler is the most recognisable historical figure of twentieth-century history. No other historical figure has aroused so much historical controversy, nor given rise to such morbid popular fascination. It is, indeed, impossible to conceive German history – and world history – taking the same course if Adolf Hitler had never lived. Yet the available evidence for Hitler's early life is extremely fragmented. Hitler's own account, offered in *Mein Kampf*, was largely inaccurate, while the very few people who knew him in the formative years of his life offered their evidence many years later, which no doubt coloured their judgement.

FAMILY BACKGROUND

Adolf Hitler (baptised as a Catholic) was born at 6.30 pm on 20 April 1889 at 'Gasthof zum Pommer', in the Austrian town of Braunau am Inn, close to the Austro-German frontier. Hitler was the fourth child of the union between Alois Hitler and Klara Poelzl. Their first three children – Gustav, Ida and Otto, all died before any of them had reached the age of three. Two more children were born after Adolf's birth: Edmond (born in 1894, but died in 1900) and Paula, born in 1896, who lived into old age. The survival of only two children, out of a family of six, was by no means abnormal in the context of the times.

Alois Hitler (Hitler's father) was born on 27 June 1837, in the small village of Strones. He was actually christened 'Alois Schicklgruber', the only son of Maria Ann Schicklgruber, the daughter of Johann Schicklgruber. The family were peasants, who had farmed land for several generations in the Waldviertal, a hilly and wooded region in the lower north west of Austria, on the border of Bohemia. At the time of his birth, Alois Hitler was termed an 'illegitimate child' because the space allotted to the father on the birth register was left blank.

A great deal of historical speculation, much of it idle, and fanciful, has been spent attempting to explain who Adolf Hitler's grandfather really was. Hitler always avoided discussing the subject, as he feared there might be some Jewish blood in his veins. The true facts still remain somewhat cloudy to this day. In 1842, Maria Schicklgruber married Johann Georg Hiedler (often spelt as 'Hitler' or 'Huttler' in the area), a fifty-year-old miller, whose family came from Spital, located about fifteen miles outside Strones. It is often assumed – quite plausibly – that Maria (who died in 1847) finally wed Johann Georg Hiedler, because he was the real father of Alois. But this has never been conclusively proven. From the time of his mother's death, perhaps even before, Alois had gone to live with Johann Nepomuk Hiedler, his father's brother (who effectively became his step-father). Even so, in 1876 Alois registered Johann Georg Hiedler (who had died nineteen years earlier) as his father, but in the birth register 'Hiedler' is spelt 'Hitler' (meaning 'smallholder'). From 1 January 1877, Alois could legally use the surname Hitler under Austrian law. This decision ensured that the future Nazi leader was not called Adolf Schicklgruber. Thousands of Germans passionately shouting 'Heil Schicklgruber' just does not sound right.

The reason for the belated change of name by Alois from Schicklgruber to Hitler has provoked much speculation among historians. One theory suggests Nepomuk wanted the name change in order to preserve the hereditary continuance of the Hiedler name, and possibly offered Alois a legacy as an inducement to change his name. A second – less plausible – theory claims Nepomuk was the 'real' father of Alois all along, which could explain why Alois went to live with him shortly after his mother's death. A third – less plausible – theory puts forward the view that neither Georg nor Nepomuk Hiedler was the father of Alois: his real father was really a 'Jew' called Frankenberger, who lived in the small Austrian village of Graz. Adolf Hitler was concerned enough about this last possibility that he asked Hans Frank, a leading Nazi, to investigate the matter during the 1930s. In a confidential report, Frank concluded that Maria Schicklgruber gave birth to Alois while she worked as a cook in the house of a 'Jewish' family called Frankenberger in Graz. The report also made the astonishing claim that Frankenberger paid maintenance for the child to Maria Schicklgruber. If this is true, then the 'Final Solution' of the 'Jewish Question' was actually ordered by someone who had Jewish blood in his veins. However, the claims in the report of Hans Frank have subsequently been shown to be untrue. To begin with, no family called Frankenberger ever lived in Graz during the 1830s, according to surviving records. There is also no evidence showing that Maria Schicklgruber ever lived or worked in Graz, and no evidence of maintenance payments being made to her. In the final analysis, the most plausible theory is the most straightforward one: Johann Georg Hiedler was the real father of

Alois. It seems his brother Nepomuk wanted this acknowledged legally before he died. Of course, there is a possibility of Nepomuk being the real father, which may help to explain why Alois lived with him for most of his life. But, if this was so, why did Alois not register Nepomuk as his real father when he had the opportunity? The answer must be that he knew all along that Georg Hiedler was his father.

PARENTS

In *Mein Kampf*, Hitler portrayed his father as a lowly customs official, who brought up his family in a state of near poverty. This was definitely untrue. Hitler's father carved out a very successful career as a well-paid, and highly respected customs official. From 1855 to 1895, Alois Hitler worked as a customs officer in several towns in Austria. He was quite frequently promoted, wore the grand uniform of a leading Hapsburg official, lived in affluent circumstances and enjoyed a salary and public status on a par with the headmaster of a private secondary school.

The private life of Alois Hitler was quite colourful – for a customs officer. He married Anna Glass in 1864, fourteen years his senior, relatively well off, but in failing health. In effect, Alois was what popular tabloids today would call a 'toy boy'. The marriage, which produced no children, was not a success, and in 1880, the couple were granted a legal separation. By this time, Alois was already in the middle of another torrid love affair with Franziska ('Fanny') Matzelberger, a very youthful maid. The couple had a son: Alois (born in 1882), and shortly after Anna Glass died (in 1883), Alois married Franziska. Only a few weeks after the wedding, Franziska gave birth to a daughter: Angela. In August 1884, however, Franziska died of tuberculosis, aged only twenty-three. Alois was not particularly overcome with grief about the untimely death of his young wife. In fact, while 'Fanny' was seriously ill, Alois had started a love affair with Klara Poelzl, his second cousin, and the granddaughter of Nepomuk Hiedler. On 7 January 1885, Alois Hitler, now aged 47, married Klara, then aged just 24. Klara was pregnant on her wedding day, and given their close family relationship, the couple needed a special dispensation from the Vatican, to allow the marriage to go ahead. Indeed, for many years after the marriage, Klara continued to address Alois as 'uncle'.

CHILDHOOD

Alois Hitler, although he moved home frequently, always provided his family with a comfortable lifestyle. Adolf Hitler, was no 'child of poverty', as he later claimed in *Mein Kampf*. He was a clean, well dressed, middle-class boy, who lived in affluent surroundings, and attended fee-paying schools. At home, there were handmade curtains on the windows, carpets on the floor, and fruit, vegetables, and a beehive producing honey in the garden. The Hitler household often included a cook and a maidservant. In Braunau am Inn (where the family lived from 1889 to 1892), the family lived in a large house with a picturesque garden. In Passau, Bavaria (from 1892 to 1895), the family home was a large apartment. From 1895 to 1897, they resided in a large country house in Hafeld, occupying nine acres of land, which had been bought from a minor Austrian nobleman. Between 1897 and 1898, the family lived in another palatial apartment in the small rural town of Lambach. In November 1898, Alois moved to another pleasant house, with a large garden in Leonding, a village on the outskirts of Linz, where he was to remain for the rest of his life. Of all the different places Adolf Hitler lived during his childhood, he always regarded the home near Linz as his favourite.

All the constant moving around, which was a feature of Hitler's childhood, meant he changed schools often, and mixed with a new and unfamiliar set of schoolmates. Adolf Hitler was a lively and able pupil, whose academic abilities were greatly hampered by his life-long dislike of hard work. At his first primary (elementary) school, at Fischlam, near Lambach (which he began on 1 May 1895), he was very popular ('a little ringleader') with his schoolmates. At this time, he found schoolwork 'ridiculously easy', leaving him 'with so much free time that the sun saw more of me than my room' (Kershaw, 1998: 15). He gained good marks in all his academic subjects, and he became an enthusiastic member of the school choir and regular churchgoer. At his next school, in Lambach, he continued to achieve good marks. At the third elementary school he attended – in Leonding – he also performed well in his first year there, but during his final year, he became introspective, sullen, moody, obstinate, and more inclined than before to go his own way. With such a generally lazy and uninterested attitude to schoolwork, his marks slipped to 'below average'. One possible reason for the sudden downturn in his mood – and his marks – during his final year at primary school may have been the sudden death (due to measles) of his younger brother Edmond.

Outside school, the young Hitler was no different from any boy of his age during this period. He enjoyed playing imaginary war games, and reading adventure stories in comics. He often led his schoolmates in rough and tumble games of cowboys and 'red Indians'. In such games, young Adolf always chose to play a red Indian (the underdog). His love of playing cowboys and Indians was inspired by reading the popular Wild West adventure stories of Karl May, a German writer, who had never even visited America. Even after Hitler became German Chancellor he was still an avid reader of May's western stories. Another passion of Hitler as a youngster was playing war games. One of Hitler's favourites was to re-enact – with his friends – the Boer struggle against the British Empire. Hitler once more was on the side of the underdogs: the Boers, the plucky and obstinate South African farmers who defied the 'mighty British Empire' between 1899 and 1902.

It would be wrong, however, to depict Hitler's childhood as completely secure and tension-free. The major source of Hitler's personal discontent as a child, notwithstanding the obvious negative psychological impact of the family's numerous house moves, and the death of other close family members, was his difficult relationship with his father. Alois Hitler was strict, frugal, humourless and extremely domineering. He was also a heavy drinker, even though his drinking never interfered with his ability to do his job. Alois demanded 'absolute obedience' at home, and he frequently punished bad behaviour with physical punishment. Hitler later recalled: 'I never loved my father. I therefore feared him all the more. He had a terrible temper and often whipped me' (Waite, 1997: 137). Hitler later described his relationship with his father as a battle of competing wills. His father wanted him to become a senior civil servant, but his headstrong young son was equally determined to become a great artist. From his father, Hitler did not receive love and guidance, only stern and domineering orders, issued, often under the threat of violence, and severely punished by violence when they were not obeyed. It is, of course, plausible to suggest Hitler's later passion for absolute domin- ance, his love of terror, can be attributed to the influence of his stern and domineering father.

If Adolf Hitler's father was a negative source of anger, his mother was definitely a compensatory positive source of love and affection in his life. Klara Hitler was a simple, quiet, uncomplicated, submissive and kind woman. Adolf Hitler had a very strong attachment to her. She watched over him as a child, pampered him, and, whenever his father was not around, let him do what he liked. In *Mein Kampf*, Hitler writes, 'I honoured my father, but I loved my mother' (Kershaw, 1998: 12). Dr Bloch, the Hitler family doctor, claimed he had 'never witnessed a closer attachment' than the one between Adolf Hitler and his mother. No other women ever compared to his mother. He even carried a picture of her in his wallet all his life. As leader of Germany, he turned his mother's birthday into a national holiday.

Adolf Hitler often referred to 'being in love with his mother', and mostly spoke of 'not liking' his father. In most 'normal' families, there is often a con- flict between a child, and one or other of its parents at various times. For the healthy development of a child, in a partnership with male and female parents, many psychiatrists believe children are more likely to avoid mental health problems in later life if they love both parents in roughly equal pro- portions. This clearly did not happen in the case of Adolf Hitler. It has been suggested he had a dysfunctional relationship with his two parents. He may even have suffered (claim some psychologists) from an 'Oedipus Complex', a theory first propounded by Sigmund Freud, which holds that when rivalry with a parent of the same sex is never resolved, and when deep love feelings towards the parent of the opposite sex are not transferred to a sexual partner outside the family, then such a person is very likely to encounter mental problems in later life. The theory has some credence when applied to Hitler, as he never did achieve a balanced relationship with both his parents, and he had few successful relationships with members of the opposite sex in later life. But whether Hitler was suffering from the 'Oedipus Complex' is psychological guesswork, based on extremely limited evidence. In any case, most of those who have been defined as suffering from such a complex, do not go on to become murderous dictators. Nor do the family circumstances of all dictators fit the theory. In fact, if we did not know of what was to come, we would surely conclude that Hitler's early childhood, in spite of some minor and unexceptional signs of emotional instability, was very ordinary, free of deprivation, and could not be remotely described as being at the extreme end of dysfunctional. As a result, writing off Hitler as a 'madman', though perhaps comforting, is a complete distortion of what he was really like.

YOUTH

On 17 September 1900, Adolf Hitler, at the age of eleven, began his secondary education at the fee-paying Realschule in Linz. The transition from primary to secondary education proved difficult, and he was extremely negative towards his educational experience from beginning to end. The journey from Leonding to school involved a three-mile walk, which took over an hour to complete.

In the small town of Leonding, Adolf Hitler, the son of a respected local civil servant, had a high status among his fellow pupils. But in Linz, a much larger town, with a population of 60,000 inhabitants, his fellow classmates, mostly composed of the sons of academics, businessmen, lawyers, doctors and people of that kind, viewed him as a rough-hewn rustic. This may help to explain why he never made any close friends at the school. It was at his secondary school that he developed, for the first time, the alienating feeling of being an 'outsider', especially among his upper-middle-class contemporaries. At the Realschule, Hitler's marks fluctuated in a range sandwiched between 'average' and 'mediocre'. His teachers viewed the young Hitler as a boy certainly not lacking in talent, but as a moody, rather lazy pupil, with a very stubborn streak. In *Mein Kampf*, Hitler claims he took a minimal interest in most academic subjects except history, geography and art; his teacher (Dr Leonard Poetsch), fired his imagination – and his growing patriotism – with vivid stories of German nationalism; he loved reading maps and free-hand drawing. Hitler claims he became a strongly emotional and passionate German nationalist during his time at secondary school. His favourite German heroes were the soldier-king Frederick the Great, and Otto von Bismarck, the first German Chancellor. Hitler claimed his poor performance at school was an act of defiance against his father's wish for him to become a civil servant when all he wanted to do was to become an artist.

On 3 January 1903, Alois Hitler collapsed and died, after suffering a lung haemorrhage while drinking red wine in a local tavern. He was buried in Leonding cemetery two days later. The death of his father, although no doubt inwardly traumatic for a young teenager to cope with, appears to have come as something of a relief to Adolf, who was now free of his father's tyranny, and able to contemplate his own dream to be 'a great artist'. With his father out of the picture, and with a doting mother, willing to indulge his whims, the teenage Adolf neglected his schoolwork like never before. He had to pass re-sit examinations in each of his remaining years at school. The headmaster of the Realschule at Linz, tired of his obvious indifference to schoolwork, forced him to move to another Realschule at Steyr, some twenty-five miles away from Linz. In September 1905, Adolf Hitler passed his final re-sit examination in geometry. This made him eligible to gain the coveted school Diploma (Abitur) after a further two years of study at a higher school: the Oberrealschule. He was not prepared to face any more schooling, and he persuaded his mother – in the autumn of 1905 – to let him leave, aged sixteen, without any qualifications. Hitler's self-inflicted failure at secondary school left him with a bitter and lifelong contempt for book-learned academics and intellectuals.

Over the next two years, Adolf Hitler became an expert in the art of loafing around. In June 1905, Klara Hitler sold the house in Leonding, and moved into a comfortable apartment in the Linz suburbs. At this stage in his life, Adolf Hitler resembled a Bohemian dilettante, with fairly long hair, a moustache, fashionable clothes, a dark hat, and always seen outside carrying a black cane, with a stylish ivory handle. He looked more like a budding Oscar Wilde than a future rabble-rousing dictator. He stayed up reading late into the wee small hours (usually books on German history, mythology and western novels), and he never got up until sometime after noon. During the day, he visited local cafés, art galleries and libraries. In the evening, he often attended the local opera house (he particularly loved Wagner) with August Kubizek, a gifted young musician, and the son of an upholsterer, who became his closest teenage friend.

The recollections of August Kubizek (or 'Gustl' as Hitler called him) are the major source for Hitler's life at this time. Kubizek's account of his friendship with Hitler was not published until 1954, and his views are somewhat clouded by his obvious admiration for the Nazi dictator.

Even so, most historians believe that Kubizek's account, in spite of its obvious deficiencies, does contain important insights into the personality of Adolf Hitler at this formative stage of his life. Hitler met Kubizek at the opera house in Linz in the autumn 1905. The relationship between these two teenagers consisted of Adolf doing most of the talking, and 'Gustl' taking the minor listening role. Hitler is described by Kubizek as 'high strung' with a tendency to 'fly off the handle' whenever conversation turned to discussions of the merits of schoolteachers, civil servants and local taxation. Kubizek did not notice Hitler holding strong anti-Semitic views or being deeply interested in politics or foreign affairs. Kubizek does mention that Hitler once came out of a performance of *Reenzi*, a Wagner opera, in 1906, claiming he would one day receive a 'mandate from the people' imploring him to lead them to 'the heights of freedom', but this sounds like Kubizek projecting on to the teenage Hitler his later political ambitions (Kubizek, 1954: 61). Hitler's greatest passions at this time were music, art and architecture. He scorned the idea of looking for a mundane job, dreaming instead of a career in the art world. To further this ambition, Hitler told 'Gustl' of his ambitious plan to try and gain entry to the illustrious Vienna Academy of Art. His determination to pursue an artistic career was strengthened further after a pleasurable holiday to the Austrian capital of Vienna in May 1906. There were, however, no girlfriends in the life of these two teenage boys. Kubizek does mention Hitler's 'infatuation' with a young upper-class girl called Stephanie, whom he had seen in Linz town centre from time to time. But Hitler admired Stephanie from afar: he wrote several 'love poems' about her, but they were never delivered. In fact, he never even spoke to her.

THE DEATH OF HIS MOTHER

The most traumatic personal event of Hitler's youth was undoubtedly the death of his beloved mother. In January 1907, Klara Hitler became seriously ill with breast cancer, and underwent a life-saving mastectomy. In the summer of 1907, with his mother still recovering from her very serious operation, Hitler persuaded her to let him go to Vienna to sit the entrance examination for the Academy of Fine Arts. For a school drop out, who had spent the previous two years in idle bliss, this was an overly ambitious plan. He rented a small flat in Vienna, sat his entrance exam in October 1907, but failed. He described the examiners as 'fossilized Bureaucrats devoid of any understanding of young talent' (Hitler, 1936: p. 20). But his examiners were right: Hitler was an artist with a talent deficit. His paintings and drawings from this period show technical competence in copying other people's works, but with no aptitude to create original works of his own. Hitler could paint and draw buildings and landscapes, but not people. Art experts – who have examined Hitler's work in detail – suggest it lacks originality, but does not reveal a personality suffering from deep psychological difficulties. Even Hitler's tendency to paint buildings rather than portraits is viewed by psychologists as the product of an introverted personality, without any deep mental difficulties.

In the meantime, the health of Hitler's mother deteriorated rapidly. In late October 1907, Hitler returned to Linz to nurse his ailing mother, night and day, during the worst period of her terminal illness. On the evening of 21 December 1907, Klara Hitler died, with Hitler loyally at her bedside to the last beat of her heart. Dr Bloch, the Jewish family doctor, who had given her close medical attention throughout her illness later commented: 'In all my career I have never seen anyone as prostrate with grief as Adolf Hitler' (Shirer, 1961: 43). The death of his mother was a dreadful blow to Hitler, as he had lost the one person he ever felt any deep affection for.

At the tender age of eighteen, Hitler had no parents and lacked emotional and financial security. In *Mein Kampf*, Hitler claims his mother's death led him to face – for the first time – the hitherto neglected problem of 'somehow making my own living' (Kershaw, 1998: 25). In reality, his financial position was not as impoverished as he later claimed. Hitler shared an inheritance from his mother of 2,000 Kronen with his sister Paula. He also received an orphan's pension of 240 Kronen per annum. In addition, he had some money left from a 924-Kronen gift from his Aunt Johanna, part of which he used to fund his first Vienna trip. Hitler was not in a comfortable position after his mother died, but he was in a better financial condition than the average student or manual labourer, and had no need to look for a job – at least for the time being.

THE VIENNA PERIOD (1908–1913)

In February 1908, Hitler returned to Vienna, where he was to remain for the next five and a half years. Vienna was one of the great cosmopolitan capitals of Europe at the time: an ethnic melting pot of Germans, Czechs, Poles, Slovaks, Serbs, Croats, Italians, Rumanians and Hungarians. It contained the largest Jewish population of any German or Austrian city. In 1910, for example, 175,318 Jews resided in Vienna, making up 8.6 per cent of the population of the metropolis. Jewish people were prominent in academia, the legal and medical professions, finance, the mass media and the arts. There was also an underclass of poor eastern European Jews who lived in the run-down parts and poverty-ridden areas of the old city.

Hitler found life in cosmopolitan, sophisticated and ethnically diverse Vienna much harder to cope with than small-town Linz, especially when he ran short of money [**Doc. 1, p. 110**]. In March 1908, Hitler was joined in the capital by his close friend 'Gustl' Kubizek, who began his studies in music at the prestigious Vienna Academy of Music. For the next few months, these two close friends from Linz shared a flat together. In this period, Kubizek saw Hitler writing poetry, sketching the outline of a play – based on German mythology – and writing a derivative Wagner-style opera (which he never completed) (Kubizek, 1954: 213). Hitler continued to visit the opera regularly and, true to form, went to bed late at night and rose late in the morning. In other words, Hitler transferred his life of blissful idleness from Linz to Vienna.

In the summer of 1908, Kubizek returned to Linz for the summer vacation. In September, Hitler took the entrance exam at the Vienna School of Arts for a second time – and failed again. He was a certainty for failure, as he had not prepared for the exam, nor had he sought any advice from the Academy about how to improve his chances in the year since his first abject failure. Even so, Hitler's failure was a shattering blow. It ended Hitler's teenage – and unrealistic – dream of becoming a 'great artist'. He slumped henceforth into a state of deep depression. In November 1908 Kubizek returned from Linz, but he found that Hitler had left the flat they shared, leaving no forwarding address.

Hitler was now alone, dependent on his own will-power. He later described his Vienna period as 'the saddest years of my life'. Yet this period of Hitler's early life, which has aroused much speculation among historians, is largely closed off to detailed historical research, owing to a severe lack of reliable sources. Hitler's own unreliable account of his Vienna years in *Mein Kampf* lacks all detail about his personal life, and attempts to portray his life as one long struggle against deprivation and poverty. Only a handful of people actually knew Hitler during this period, and even those who did know him, recorded their views of him much later, thus distorting any understanding of what he was really like at the time.

Hitler's rejection by the Vienna art establishment was a great blow to his self-esteem. It made him very bitter, plunging him into a state of depression. Hitler had desperately wanted – although he later tried to deny it – to be accepted into the bourgeois traditional art elite at the Academy of Arts. Hitler always felt superior to people from a working-class background, and he was 'determined' not to slip down the social scale – as he saw it – and become associated with that class. As a result, Hitler was determined to avoid taking any job associated with the working classes in general and anything that involved hard manual work in particular. One person who met Hitler during his Vienna period later told of how he would often show a picture of his late father, wearing the grand uniform of the Imperial Customs Service, in order to emphasise – in a rather insecure manner – his middle-class background and its supposed 'respectability'.

Hitler had no desire to look for a mundane job, and he did not want to return to Linz as a failure. So he stayed in Vienna, unsure of what to do with the rest of his life. He made no effort to gain a full-time job, nor did he come forward to undertake his compulsory military service in the Austrian armed forces – as he was legally obliged to do – in the summer of 1909. From the autumn of 1908 until the late summer months of 1909, he lived in three different flats. In the mild autumn of 1909, he briefly lived rough, mostly sleeping on park benches. Exactly why he needed to live in this way remains unclear. One possibility is that Hitler's savings from his inheritance finally ran out. A more convincing explanation as to why Hitler slept rough in the autumn of 1909 was his knowledge that he was now eligible for conscription into the Austrian army. In sum, Hitler's brief period as a 'down and out' in Vienna, which lasted less than three months, was really a means of avoiding being conscripted into the army.

In October 1909, Hitler took up residence in the Meidling, a men's hostel, funded by a wealthy Jewish family. We also know he undertook a few odd jobs at this time: cleared some snow; carried luggage for passengers at a local railway station, and worked for a couple of days as a building labourer. At the hostel he was befriended by Reinhold Hanisch, an unemployed ex-domestic servant, and 'artist', perhaps, of the bar-room variety. Hanisch described Hitler when he first caught sight of him as shabbily dressed and incapable of organising his own life. Hanisch persuaded him to write a letter to one of his relatives for some money to buy artists' materials, and then set himself up as a commercial artist. Hanisch promised to sell Hitler's paintings and postcards in return for a commission on each sale. Hitler did write to his ever-loyal aunt Johanna, who sent him 50 Kronen by return of post. With this money, Hitler bought an overcoat and some artists' materials.

In December 1909, Hitler – accompanied by Hanisch – moved to the Männerheim, a much smarter lodging house, occupied by working men on limited incomes. The residents of this 'Home for Men' paid nearly 3 Kronen a week for a small room (which had to be vacated during working hours). In return, they gained access to the many other facilities on offer, which included a large dining room, a reading room, a shower room, and a laundry. As Hitler was not allowed to paint in his own room, he did so on a small table by a window in the lounge area. This was, of course, a great come-down for someone who had aspired to become a 'great artist'. Yet Hitler's time at the Männerheim actually strengthened his personality and infused him with a belief that life was a constant struggle in which only those with great will-power and strength of character could hope to survive.

Those who knew Hitler at the Männerheim – from 1909 to 1913 – later described him as a 'loner', who held extremely dogmatic opinions on almost every subject imaginable. While he stayed at the hostel, he completed between

700 and 800 paintings, drawings and postcards, most of which were copied from other people's work, and sold in nearby shops, taverns, cafés and art shops. In addition, he produced several advertising posters for local businesses, including one for an antiperspirant foot powder called 'Teddy's'.

By the end of 1910, Hitler – it is estimated – was earning 70 to 80 Kronen a month from the sales of his artwork. There are also strong indications that his income was further boosted by a substantial gift of 3,800 Kronen from his aunt Johanna. A further sign of his healthy financial state was his decision to transfer his orphan's pension (which he had fraudulently continued to receive by claiming he was a 'student' at the Vienna School of Art) of 24 Kronen per month to his half-sister, Angela.

However, the partnership between Hitler and the streetwise Hanisch lasted only eight months. It ended because Hitler thought his painting of the Vienna Parliament building had been sold for fifty crowns, not the ten crowns which Hanisch claimed he had received for it. Hitler felt he had been cheated and he took legal proceedings against Hanisch. During the hearing of the case – which took place on 11 August 1910 – Hitler claimed Hanisch was 'a practiced liar' who was registered at the Mannerheim under the false name of Fritz Walter. At the end of the court proceedings, Hanisch was sentenced to seven days in jail. In the 1930s Hanisch sold the story of his brief and tempestuous relationship with Hitler to the popular press. In 1936, Hanisch was arrested by the Gestapo, and charged with spreading 'libellous stories about Hitler'. On 4 February 1937, he was found dead in his cell, reportedly from a 'heart attack', but there are strong indications he was murdered by the Gestapo (probably on Hitler's orders).

HITLER'S POLITICAL IDEAS IN VIENNA

In *Mein Kampf*, Hitler claimed he was keenly interested in the political developments in Vienna. But he belonged to no political party and kept up to date on political matters by reading newspapers, periodicals and cheap pamphlets. His major interests were in the less openly political areas of music, art and architecture. It seems Hitler's political views in this period were pretty similar to those of upper-class elites and lower-middle-class groups who felt threatened by the growth of socialist ideas. Before Hitler came to Vienna, he was certainly a fervent nationalist, who identified with the Protestant German Reich rather than the multi-national Hapsburg Empire, even though he was himself a Catholic.

Hitler later claimed two political figures had a profound influence upon his political 'awakening' in Vienna: Georg von Shroenerer, leader of the Pan-German Nationalist Party, and Karl Lueger, the leader of the Christian Social

Party. Shroenerer's Pan-German Party, unlike its German equivalent, was not preoccupied with German imperial expansion outside Europe, but instead championed the idea of all Germans living in a single state. Shroenerer was deeply anti-Semitic, regarding 'the Jews' as responsible for all the evils of the world, and demanding special 'anti-Jewish laws' to prevent the further growth of Jewish influence in Austrian society. The major weaknesses of Shroenerer as a politician, according to Hitler, were his inability to arouse – or even seek – the support of the masses and his complete failure to gain support for his political ideas from the powerful institutions of the state: the army, the church and the bureaucracy.

It was Dr Karl Lueger, the popular leader of the Christian Social Party and mayor of Vienna, who made an even greater impression on the young Hitler. It was not the political programme of this Austrian demagogue which attracted Hitler. In fact, he thought Lueger had too much faith in the Austrian multi-national state, and did not champion German nationalist ideas passionately enough. What Hitler admired most about Lueger were his oratorical abilities and his pragmatic approach to political problems. Lueger was a populist leader, who pursued his political objectives in a pragmatic and flexible manner. He was willing to exploit ideologies – in order to win over voters – some of which he did not believe in. The group he aimed his oratory towards as mayor of Vienna were the backbone of the lower-middle class: white-collar workers, Catholic workers, artisans, local government officials and shopkeepers, but his oratory also proved attractive to sections of the upper-middle class, who were usually attracted to conservative parties. Above all, Hitler was impressed by Lueger's ability to appeal to the ordinary voter through powerful slogans such as 'We must do something for the Little Man!'

Hitler was already a fervent anti-Marxist during his time in Vienna. He had a 'great hatred' of the Social Democrat Party, because of the devotion of its supporters towards socialist ideas. Yet there were aspects of the socialist left he did admire, particularly the ability of the Social Democratic Party to make effective use of propaganda to attract the masses and their ability to go out on the streets in demonstrations and parades, carrying flags and banners to emphasise the strength and unity of their supporters. Hitler believed only by challenging the socialists 'on the streets' could they be stopped from winning over the masses to their ideas.

Hitler claimed in *Mein Kampf* that the idea of combining the extreme German nationalism of Shroenerer, with the charismatic leadership of Lueger, and the popular street fighting and propaganda abilities of the socialists to form a 'National Socialist' Party was already forming in his mind during his period in Vienna. It is clear such a party was primarily viewed – by Hitler – as a popular alternative to the rise of socialist ideas. Yet we only have Hitler's word that his political ideas were so clear at this time in his life. It is probably more accurate to suggest these views about his political ideas in Vienna were self-serving rhetoric, designed to portray himself as a man of crystal clear vision, when in reality Hitler had no independently thought-out political ideas of his own. In reality, Hitler was an interested spectator of politics in Vienna, who had not even contemplated a career in politics.

HITLER'S ANTI-SEMITISM IN VIENNA

It is also important to assess Hitler's views towards 'the Jews' during his Vienna period, given the importance of these ideas in the later history of the Nazi Party. Surprisingly, there is little evidence in Hitler's early life to suggest that an ingrained prejudice against 'the Jews' was a dominant pre-occupation. On the contrary, the sincere feelings Hitler expressed towards Dr Bloch, a Jewish doctor, for the care he had offered his mother during her terminal illness does not indicate a congenital hatred of all Jewish people. Hitler admits to being tolerant of Jews while he lived in Linz, often expressing 'repugnance' whenever he heard strong expressions of anti-Semitism. On the other hand, Kubizek, his close friend, does recall Hitler being somewhat prejudiced against Jews in Linz, and Vienna, but does not think he was an extreme anti-Semite during the time he knew him [**Doc. 1, p. 110**].

It was during his Vienna period when Hitler's views towards the Jews started to change. According to Hitler, he went from being a 'weak kneed cosmopolitan' to a 'fanatical anti-Semite' during his Vienna period (Fest, 1974: 39). What prompted Hitler's growing hatred towards the Jews is a subject of deep historical significance. Hitler claimed his rising resentment towards Jews was – at first – prompted by seeing Jews 'everywhere' on the streets of Vienna and concluding they had 'no resemblance to Germans' [**Doc. 1, p. 110**]. This visual dislike of the Jew as an 'alien' force in Vienna was strongly reinforced by Hitler's subsequent reading of many popular anti-Semitic pamphlets and newspapers. Hitler appears to have swallowed whole the prevailing views of this cheap anti-Semitic literature, which blamed the Jews for every sin and vice in multi-cultural Vienna. One key aspect of the gutter anti-Semitic press in Vienna was its continual stress on Jews being heavily involved in running the vice trade in the city. Anti-Semitic pamphlets were full of stories of 'racially unfit' Jews 'seducing innocent German maidens'.

It has been suggested that one of the roots of Hitler's virulent anti-Semitism may have been a tortured sexual envy, prompted by seeing Jewish men – even of advancing years – seducing young girls, whom Hitler did not even have the courage to talk to. Hitler's sexual relations in Vienna are a mystery. One person who met Hitler during his Vienna period – and whose evidence is considered very unreliable – suggested Hitler had sex with prostitutes in

Vienna, and was obsessed with defecation and urination as part of the sex act. Yet another witness from the Vienna period – equally unreliable – claims Hitler attempted, unsuccessfully, to rape a young model, while she was posing in a life-drawing class. More recently, Lothar Machtan, a German historian, has controversially argued that Hitler was a (repressed) homosexual, who had sex with 'rent boys' during his Vienna period (Machtan, 2001). It is, however, far more likely that Hitler had no sexual contact with either men or women during his entire time in Vienna.

Another possibility, and a more plausible one, is that a virulent, all-consuming anti-Semitism did not dominate Hitler's political – or sexual – thinking during his Vienna period. Hitler was certainly attracted to anti-Semitic ideas during his Vienna period, but this was true of the majority of supporters of German nationalism. It is more doubtful that Hitler's anti-Semitism was an all-consuming 'master idea' at that juncture in his life. For a so-called 'passionate' anti-Semite, some of Hitler's behaviour in Vienna was extremely odd. Hitler regularly attended musical evenings at the home of a Jewish family. Most of his closest acquaintances at the Mannerheim, including those he most trusted, were Jewish. It is also known he preferred to sell his paintings through Jewish art dealers, because he regarded them as the most honest to deal with.

MUNICH (1913–1914)

In May 1913, Adolf Hitler, then aged twenty-four, suddenly ended his lonely and very unsuccessful period in Vienna. He travelled by train across the Austrian border to the German city of Munich. Hitler's fateful relationship with Germany and its people had now begun. Yet a patriotic love of Germany was not the major reason for his departure from the Austrian capital. Hitler – who had successfully avoided conscription for over four years – feared he was about to be called up for military service. He registered with the Munich police as 'stateless' rather than as an 'Austrian citizen' as he was legally required to do. The documents relating to Hitler's failure to enlist in the army show that the Austrian military authorities had been searching in vain for him for some considerable time. Hitler had never presented himself at any time to undertake his military service from 1909 to 1913. Police files relating to the case reveal that he had not registered his address in Vienna with the police in Linz. The police eventually discovered he had gone to live in Vienna from interviews with people in Linz who knew him. The police soon made inquiries at the Mannerheim and found out he had already left there for Munich. In January 1914, the Austrian police finally tracked him down – with the assistance of the German criminal police – to a Munich address (34 Schleissheimer Strasse), located in a poor area of the city, where he had taken lodgings with the family of Joseph Popp, a tailor, at a cost of 20 marks a month. The charge of 'draft dodging' (most famously associated later with American peace-loving 'hippies' in the 1960s) was a very serious one in Austria in 1914, and carried a lengthy prison sentence. Hitler was asked to go to Salzburg (on 5 February 1914) to explain why he had avoided service for so long. In a written statement, presented to the recruitment board, Hitler claimed he had not come forward for military service in the autumn of 1909 because he was 'a very inexperienced man, without any financial aid' and 'no other companion but eternally gnawing hunger'. He also claimed he had submitted his documents for military service, but they must have been lost in the post. Of course, these explanations were extremely weak. There is little doubt he deliberately – and consciously – avoided military service. Yet the Salzburg recruitment panel accepted his explanation. In the end, they decided Hitler was 'unfit' and 'too weak' for military service because of a minor lung complaint. Hitler later claimed he was a 'draft dodger', not because he was a coward – or, more likely, plain lazy – but because did not want to join the Austrian army, as he felt great animosity towards the Austro-Hungarian empire and a greater affinity for Germany.

Hitler describes the brief time he spent in Munich before the First World War as 'the happiest and by far the most contented of my life' (Bullock, 1962: 48). Munich enjoyed the reputation before 1914 of being a charming, artistic, light-hearted and culturally open city. Hitler's life in Munich followed much the same shapeless pattern as it had done in Vienna. He remained without close friends and made no contacts with the art world or local political groups. Hitler liked Munich because it was a 'German city', very different from ethnically diverse Vienna.

The members of the Popp family, with whom Hitler lived, later recalled Hitler as leading a solitary existence. He mostly painted postcards and watercolours, which he sold to local dealers. He also borrowed many books from the local library. Hitler was able to command an income of 120 marks per month, a modest income but one which allowed him to live tolerably. During the day, he would also sit, reading newspapers in local cafés, mostly drinking coffee, and occasionally indulging in his life-long love of chocolate cake. By this time, Hitler appears to have realised he was not going to be a great artist. He painted to earn a modest living, and planned to pursue academic studies in order to become an architect.

THE FIRST WORLD WAR

The event which truly transformed Hitler's life was the outbreak of the First World War. 'I am not ashamed to say', Hitler later wrote in *Mein Kampf*, 'carried away by the enthusiasm of the moment, I sank down on my knees and thanked heaven out of the fullness of my heart for granting me the good fortune of being permitted to live in such a time' (Toland, 1976: 46). Many historians view Hitler as a logical consequence of deep-seated flaws in German historical development. Yet Hitler's rise to power was more a consequence of the German defeat in the First World War than anything else. Without the war – and the fact that Germany lost it – it is almost certain Hitler would never have entered politics and the Nazi Party would never have needed to exist.

Hitler volunteered on 3 August 1914 to serve in the German army. He was accepted by the 16th Bavarian Infantry Regiment (known as the 'List' Regiment), in spite of his Austrian citizenship, and he spent most of the war – on the Western front – as a dispatch runner carrying messages between the officer staff at H.Q. and front-line troops. Hitler was not a soldier in the trenches, but his job, a solitary one – which suited his personality – was hazardous. Many dispatch riders (usually riding bicycles, but sometimes motorcycles in the latter stages of the war) were killed by enemy fire while trying to deliver their vital messages.

Hitler's extremely passionate involvement with the fate of the German army during the First World War was the real turning point in his life. Hitler describes his period in the German army during the 'Great War' as 'the most memorable period of my life' (Bullock, 1962: 50). The war not only gave Hitler a means of showing his nationalist passion for the German cause, but also offered him the opportunity to escape from boredom, frustration and failure. It gave his life a new purpose and energy: he was now a soldier fighting for the country he loved.

The army was for Hitler a surrogate home and family. During the war, Hitler claimed he had no worries. He took orders from officers without a word of comment, nor did he ever question the decisions taken by his officers or the aims of the war. Whenever he heard of acts of humanity displayed by German soldiers towards the enemy (such as the famous 1914 Christmas Day football match in no man's land between British and German soldiers) he expressed outrage. He was respected by his officers as 'loyal and obedient'.

His fellow soldiers in the List Regiment thought 'Adi' (their nickname for him) an 'eccentric'. They noticed he could often sit for hours, silently brooding, or reading, but would occasionally jump to his feet and break into a 'wild monologue', usually bemoaning anyone who showed a lack of patriotism towards the German war effort. He never complained about the mud, the filth and the lack of food on the front line. One certain way of hearing Hitler's loudest angry rhetoric was to suggest Germany might actually lose the war. Many fellow soldiers, though not completely disliking him, often found his unquestioning patriotism irritating. As a fellow soldier put it: 'We cursed him and found him intolerable' (Shirer, 1961: 48). Hitler never asked for leave, did not receive letters from home (not even at Christmas) and never gave any details of his early life to fellow soldiers. He would often shake his head when hearing light-hearted remarks or jokes. He was not at all interested, when on leave, in seeking the company of women or engaging in the sexual banter that was then commonplace among his fellow soldiers. His closest companion during the war was a stray dog he adopted called 'Foxl'. On political matters, his fellow soldiers claimed he had very little to say. No soldier can remember him mentioning his so-called 'ingrained anti-Semitism'. Photographs taken of Hitler during the war show him with a dour, fixed expression on his face. He appears isolated from his fellow soldiers, and looks much older than his mid-twenties.

Yet, it must be admitted that Hitler was a very good soldier. His coolness under fire earned him a reputation of 'invulnerability' from his fellow soldiers. In December 1914, he was awarded the Iron Cross medal (Second Class). In August 1918, he received the Iron Cross (First Class). The latter award, given on the recommendation of a Jewish officer, was a very prestigious award, rarely given to a volunteer soldier. Accounts vary as to why Hitler received it. One account claims he took fifteen British soldiers prisoner. But the official history of the List Regiment gives no details about the specific act of bravery for which it was awarded. The award of the Iron Cross was very important for Hitler's later political career as a German nationalist. It gave tangible evidence of his bravery. Given his obvious devotion to duty, it is surprising he was never promoted above the rank of lance corporal. A senior officer of the List Regiment – in evidence at the Nuremberg war trials – said the question of promoting Hitler did often crop up, but he was rejected because 'we could discover no leadership qualities in him' (Fest, 1974: 69).

In October 1916, Hitler was wounded in the left thigh during the Battle of the Somme. He was sent to Beelitz hospital in Berlin to recover from his injury. In Berlin, after his discharge from the hospital, he noticed people 'boasting of their own cowardice' and a general atmosphere of discontent and defeatism. On a visit to Munich shortly afterwards he 'could no longer recognise the city' and noticed 'every clerk was a Jew' (Hitler, 1936: 87). He became increasingly filled with fury against politicians, journalists, Jews and left-wing radicals who were constantly talking of defeat. Hitler returned to the front, convinced the German war effort was being severely undermined by 'Jews and Marxists' at home.

Hitler took part in the final offensive of the German army in 1918. On the evening of 18 October 1918, south of Ypres, Hitler was briefly blinded in a mustard gas attack, and was transported to Pasewalk hospital in Pomerania to recover. In November 1918, a pastor told patients that a revolution had broken out in Germany, the Kaiser had abdicated, a republic declared, and the war had been lost. On hearing this news, Hitler – for the first time since he stood over his mother's grave – began to cry. 'It became impossible for me to sit still one minute more', Hitler later recalled, 'And everything went black again before my eyes. I tottered and groped my way back to the dormitory, threw myself on my bunk, and dug my burning head into my blanket and pillow . . . So it had all been in vain' (Fest, 1974: 78).

Hitler later claimed this was the exact moment when he decided to enter politics, in order to rid Germany of the 'wretched gang of Socialists, Jews, and democratic politicians who had stabbed Germany in the back' and robbed it of victory. The end of the war was also a very personal blow to Hitler. It meant he had no work, no home, no friends and no job. In reality, Hitler – fully aware of the powerlessness of his position – had not really made up his mind to enter politics as soon as he heard of Germany's defeat. All he had decided to do, since he had nowhere else to go, nor any real idea of what the future held, was to stay in the army, even though the army in Bavaria at the time was run by the 'Soldiers Councils' he supposedly despised. When he did take his first active steps into politics, over a year after the war ended, it was on the orders of an army officer. As with most of the acts of Hitler's early life, the reality was very different from the myth.

3

The Early Growth of the Nazi Party, 1918–1924

On 21 November 1918, Hitler returned to Munich in a dispirited state of mind to contemplate an uncertain future. When he arrived, Munich was in a state of political crisis. The Wittelsbach monarchy, a feature of Bavarian political life for a thousand years, had already been toppled. The Bavarian People's Republic, composed of a group of socialist revolutionaries led by Kurt Eisner, a diminutive, bearded, Jewish, Social Democrat, promised 'government by kindness'. A sizeable number of the leading personalities in the new government were Jewish intellectuals, strongly attached to Marxist ideals. It might be expected that Hitler, given his supposed bitter anti-Marxist and Semitic views, would have nothing to do with this type of socialist rule, and engage in counter-revolutionary activities. Yet he did nothing of the sort. In fact, Hitler tolerated the new socialist – and Jewish-dominated – Bavarian government, for a personal, selfish and opportunistic reason: he wanted to stay in the army. It did not seem to matter to him that the Munich regiment in which he served was under the control of a left-wing 'Soldiers' Council'. It was not the first, nor would it be the last occasion, when Hitler would compromise his so-called 'unshakable principles' in order to do what he wanted.

The 'socialist experiment' in Munich, built on the extraordinary revolutionary mood that swept through Germany at the end of the First World War, soon collapsed. The new government favoured democratic rule, but did not purge nationalist and anti-democratic groups within the army, the civil service, the police force and the judiciary. As a result, the forces of the Bavarian right regrouped. On 21 February 1919, Eisner, while walking to the Bavarian parliament, was gunned down by a young right-wing Munich University student, with aristocratic connections: Graf Anton von Arco-Valley. This provocative political assassination prompted communist leaders to call a general strike. In April, the socialists established a communist-style 'Soviet Council' led by Rudolf Eglhofer, and his 'Red Army'. The level of violence between left and right in Bavaria intensified.

On 29 April 1920, eight prisoners of the 'Red Army', including some members of the right wing Thule Society, were brutally murdered. This crime galvanised most of the right-wing elements in Bavarian society into an explosive counter-reaction. The result was a four-day 'mini Civil War' during which troops from the Red Army, supported by the Free Corps (Freikorps), consisting of hundreds of patriotic, wild-eyed, trigger-happy ex-soldiers, armed with hand grenades and rifles – supplied from army stocks – quickly suppressed the short-lived workers' revolt in a bloody struggle that left most of the communist leaders (among them Eglhofer) wounded or dead. The final death toll in this brief, but bloody Bavarian conflict was 606 dead, including 335 civilians. Most of these were communists and socialists. A 'moderate' Social Democrat (SPD) government was put back in power. But this was swiftly replaced by an extreme right-wing nationalist government led by Gustav von Kahr, supported by the reactionary local leaders of the German army.

THE BIRTH OF THE NAZI PARTY

After the demise of the 'red dictatorship', everything changed in Bavarian politics. The region became a right-wing Noah's Ark, in which every type of snarling nationalist found refuge. Hitler, although he took no active part in crushing the left in Bavaria, was now in the perfect place to make his mark on the political stage. It must be understood, however, that Hitler's first move into politics was not even his own idea. In May 1919, he was selected by Captain Karl Mayr to become an Instruction Officer in the Information Department of the district command of the army. Mayr later described Hitler as 'a stray dog looking for a master . . . ready to throw in his lot with anyone who would show him kindness' (Kershaw, 1998: 122). The Information Department had been given government funding to create a group of reliable pro-nationalist agents whose main task was to indoctrinate officers and soldiers with nationalist and anti-communist ideas. In June 1919, Hitler was sent by his army superiors on a week-long course on 'anti-Bolshevism' at Munich University. During the course, Hitler heard a number of pro-nationalist lectures, including one that greatly impressed him: 'breaking interest slavery' delivered by Gottfried Feder, a Pan-German economics lecturer who told the students that 'productive capital' in large German-run industries should be encouraged, but 'rapacious capital' which he associated with 'Jews' should be 'eliminated' from the German economy. It seems Hitler made a favourable impression with Feder on the course, as he told Mayr shortly afterwards about Hitler's 'natural' speaking abilities, displayed during the discussion sessions which followed each lecture. In August 1919, Hitler, given the role of 'Educational Officer' by Mayr, was asked to 'instruct' troops on a five-day course at a local army camp on the dangers of communism. On this course, Hitler discovered his greatest talent: he was an excellent, dramatic and passionate speaker, with a popular manner that immediately struck a chord with his listeners. It was the realisation of his natural ability as a public speaker that first propelled Hitler towards the idea of becoming actively engaged in politics.

In September 1919, Mayr gave Hitler the task of spying on the many small right- and left-wing political parties and radical debating societies operating in the Munich area during this fraught period. Hitler was 'ordered' by Mayr to go and observe a gathering of the German Workers' Party (**Deutsche Arbeiterpartei – DAP**), held in a Munich Beer Hall (the Sterneckbrau). The DAP had been set up by Anton Drexler, a locksmith, working for a rail company, and Karl Harrer, a local right-wing journalist. The party first appeared at the end of the First World War as 'The "Workers" Political Society', a small discussion group, with a restricted member ship of just seven people. Drexler wanted the group to become a political party, which appealed to the public. On 5 January 1919, therefore, the DAP became a political party, which started to organise meetings, and was always on the lookout for new members.

The small inner core of activists in the DAP mostly met in the small, dimly lit back rooms of beer halls. The DAP struck a strongly nationalist, anti-Semitic and anti-capitalist tone. It had a democratic constitution: the membership elected the executive committee, discussions took place on policy issues, and votes decided the party line adopted. Yet the DAP, led by Drexler, lacking in funds and members, stood little chance of becoming a major political party. The first time Hitler attended a meeting of the DAP, on Friday 12 September 1919, the keynote speaker was Gottfried Feder, who gave the lecture on 'interest slavery', which Hitler had already heard before at Munich University. In the brief discussion which followed, Professor Baumann, the second invited speaker, suggested it would be a good idea for Bavaria to break away from Germany. This prompted Hitler to launch a strong verbal attack on Baumann's views. Drexler was so impressed by Hitler's impressive interjection in the debate that he made the point of going up to him at the end of the meeting, invited him to join the party, took his name and address, then pressed a copy of his self-penned pamphlet: 'My Political Awakening' into his hand [**Doc. 2, p. 110**]. Once more, it was Hitler's brilliant speaking ability that had caught the eye and impressed the listener.

Hitler was not impressed by what he saw at the poorly attended meeting of the DAP. It was little different in its political stance from many similar *Volkisch* nationalist groups, operating in Munich at the time. Hitler was more attracted by Drexler's pamphlet, which he read, unable to sleep, just before dawn, on the following morning. It told the story of how this humble locksmith had created a new political party, combining nationalism with some anti-capitalist and 'socialist' ideas. Yet the major aim of the party was

Deutsche Arbeiterpartei **(DAP):** The German Workers' Party, founded by Anton Drexler, a Munich locksmith. It was this party which Hitler joined and which later became the Nazi Party.

Volkisch: racial: ethnic: nationalist.

to weaken the appeal of Marxism and socialism among the working classes. Hitler claimed he was already thinking of creating a political party along similar lines, even before he went to observe the meeting of the DAP. Hence, when a postcard arrived, a few days after the meeting he had attended, inviting him to join the Committee of the DAP, he accepted. Hitler later claimed he decided to join because he thought this small, ill-organised, and little-known party, could be moulded to suit his own purposes. According to the Hitler myth, he was the seventh member of the party, but when his membership card was later found in the German archives, it was discovered his membership number was 515.

Hitler's own subjective account about his motivation for joining the DAP must also be treated with great caution. His claim about wrestling with nagging doubts before joining the party hardly seem credible when all the facts are considered. Mayr, his army boss, whose account is far more reliable, says he 'ordered' Hitler to join so the party could be used as a propaganda vehicle for the army to bolster its drive to weaken the appeal of socialism among the workers. It also seems clear that army funds, probably channelled through Hitler after he joined the party, were used to enable Hitler to book local halls as speaking venues for the party, and to finance expensive newspaper advertisements. In fact, during Hitler's early active period as a member of the DAP from September 1919 to April 1920 he continued to draw his army salary, and he stopped his surveillance activities on other right- and left-wing parties. This suggests the army had decided to 'plant' Hitler in the DAP to build up its popularity. It seems reasonable to conclude, therefore, that it was Mayr and his fellow officers who decided the DAP's novel combination of nationalism and socialism could be used as a suitable army vehicle – under Hitler's leadership – for its own anti-socialist propaganda. No doubt other 'political instructors' made their way into the Nazi Party – and other right-wing parties – under similar orders. We know, for example, that Hermann Esser, Mayr's press agent, became an important speaker and propagandist in the early Nazi Party. Hitler's move into politics was really the result of an order from the army, not part of a fully thought-out plan of his own. Accordingly, Hitler began his career in politics as a willing tool of anti-democratic forces within the Munich command of the army.

Hitler now had a field of action for his passionate love of Germany, his propaganda skill and, especially, his brilliant speaking ability. Hitler's entry into politics gave him a new lease of life. He immediately – and energetically – threw himself into his role as the chief propagandist of the infant party. Within a matter of weeks, Hitler transformed the DAP from a German lounge bar ranting club, into a noisy local nationalist party, fond of creating a public outcry. On 16 October 1919, Hitler organised a public meeting of the DAP, attended by 111 people.

Hitler's speeches at subsequent public meetings helped to increase the profile and membership of the party. It was not what Hitler said – most right-wing hot heads said much the same – but the way he said it: in a manner reminiscent of fundamentalist religious fanatics, evoking melancholy images of suffering and despair, willing to give his life for a cause, which set him apart as a public speaker, put the Nazi Party on the map of local Munich politics, and salvaged Hitler from a career that seemed to be heading for the graveyard of under-achievers.

In his speeches, Hitler cast himself in the role an alienated, bitter and resentful 'outsider' from the 'new Germany'. He had the unique ability to inspire an audience to share his bitterness, his fears, his self-pity, and his frustrations, and he also inspired them to support his 'positive' programme to rescue the Germans from the 'cowards and traitors' who had 'betrayed the Fatherland' [Doc. 9, p. 117]. In doing so, Hitler gave his listeners a dream that 'tomorrow belonged to them'. Hitler built up this idealism for a better tomorrow on the foundation of deep feelings of unhappiness and bitterness over the German defeat in the war. He blamed that defeat on those people at home who he claimed had 'stabbed Germany in the back'. Every ex-soldier, still depressed about Germany's defeat, and in sympathy with nationalist ideas, could easily identify with Hitler's outbursts of loathing against the 'November criminals', 'the profiteering Jews' and the Treaty of Versailles [Doc. 4, p. 113]. All of Hitler's speeches built towards a feverish, hysterical, climax, usually ending with the phrase: 'There is only defiance and hate, hate and again hate'.

Hitler soon became indispensable to this small right-wing fringe party. He was not only the most effective public speaker in the party, but its most effective organiser and propagandist. He put the party on a more businesslike footing, by renting an office above the Sternecker Beer Hall, installing in it a telephone, a safe, filing cabinet and a typewriter. A rubber stamp, bearing the party name, and printed membership cards were also purchased. A great deal of effort was made by Hitler to improve the advertising of the party. Hitler was involved in designing striking red posters and leaflets for the party, which were posted around Munich.

It was also Hitler who insisted the party should take its message to larger audiences, something older members of the party committee were not very enthusiastic about doing. The large gatherings of the party were never peaceful. On the contrary, they provoked confrontation with left-wing opponents, generated passion from supporters, and injected the much-needed oxygen of publicity into the party. A substantial proportion of young people were attracted to meetings of the party by action, excitement and the many opportunities for violence they offered.

On 24 February 1920, one of the first large meetings of party, held at the Hofbrauhaus, which Hitler had publicised through advertising in the local press, attracted an audience of 2,000 people. At the meeting, Hitler outlined the twenty-five-point party programme, drafted by Feder, Drexler and Hitler [**Doc. 3, p. 111**]. Not long after the meeting, the DAP changed its name to the National Socialist German Workers Party (***Nationalsozialistische Deutsche Arbeiterpartei – NSDAP***), and became commonly known as the Nazi Party, adopting as its party symbol, under Hitler's insistence, the now infamous swastika. On 1 April 1920, Hitler finally left the army, with the intention of seizing the leadership of the Nazi Party, and making it the instrument of his own particular brand of extreme nationalism.

THE EARLY PROGRAMME OF THE NAZI PARTY

Nationalsozialistische Deutsche Arbeiterpartei (**NSDAP**): The National Socialist German Workers Party, the full title of the Nazi Party. The party grew rapidly in support from 1928 onwards to become the most popular political party in Germany at the time when Hitler came to power.

The twenty-five points of the Nazi Party were declared 'unalterable', but were mostly ignored when Hitler came to power. The Party's most notable gimmick was to combine right-wing, nationalist and anti-Semitic ideas, with some anti-capitalist, so-called 'socialist' measures. This novel combination allowed the Nazi Party a banner under which workers could shelter along-side middle- and upper-class groups, thereby providing an effective bulwark against communist revolution at home and offering the possibility of restoring German military power in the world.

The 'national' elements of the party programme included promises to revise the 'hated' Treaty of Versailles, unite all German speakers into an expanded Greater German Reich, exclude Jews from 'German' citizenship rights, take control of the press, and build a 'strong' nationalist government under the direction of an all-powerful leader. The 'socialist' parts of the platform included pledges to nationalise trusts, abolish land rents, restrict interest on loans, introduce profit sharing in industry, open up large depart-ment stores to small traders, confiscate profits made by industry during war, and create a People's Army [**Doc. 3, p. 111**]. The 'anti-capitalist' elements on the programme appeared to spell the end of interest-bearing loans. One striking omission was the complete neglect – apart from a brief mention of land reform – of the plight of agriculture. The broad principles of the party programme were never substantially challenged or altered during the period of the Nazi rise to power.

The 'nationalist' parts of the programme were not dissimilar to those championed by other nationalist groups. But they were – for the most part – supported by Hitler, who implemented many of them after he came to power. What really distinguished the Nazi Party platform from other right-wing fringe groups – and gave it a distinctive appeal – was its advocacy of certain so-called 'socialist' and 'anti-capitalist' policies. These proposed 'socialist' measures were supported by many members of the party. But Hitler viewed most of them as mere window dressing, designed to attract 'dumb' workers to the party. This view is reinforced by the knowledge that hardly any of the 'socialist' elements of the Nazi Party programme were ever implemented after 1933. Hitler was quite prepared – as his time in the 'Information Department' of the army had taught him – to use the slogans and symbols of socialism to gain support for extreme nationalism.

THE EMERGENCE OF HITLER AS LEADER OF THE NAZI PARTY

By the end of 1920, Nazi membership grew to 3,000, largely as a result of Hitler's public speeches, and his energetic propaganda efforts. In December 1920, the Nazi Party bought a local newspaper (the *Münchener Beobachter*) for 180,000 marks, renaming it soon afterwards as the **Völkischer Beobachter** (**Racial Observer**). The large sum of money used to buy the official party newspaper came from Eckart, some prominent Munich conservatives, and a 60,000 mark donation from secret army funds. It was the purchase of the *Völkischer Beobachter* that greatly increased Hitler's dominance over the party, as he used the paper as the chief agency of party propaganda, and as a means of transmitting orders and directives to local party activists.

Völkischer Beobachter: *Racial Observer*. The official Nazi Party newspaper. It is now known that army secret funds helped to finance the purchase of this newspaper.

At this time, Hitler had surrounded himself with a team of people who became the nucleus of the Nazi Party leadership, most notably: Alfred Rosenberg, the self-styled party philosopher, who championed the racial theories of the party, especially its pronounced anti-Semitic views; Max Amann, Hitler's former army sergeant, who became the publishing manager; Dietrich Eckart, a poet and publicist with a severe alcohol problem, provided Hitler with much-needed funding and contacts; Captain Ernst Röhm (introduced to Hitler by Mayr), a tough and menacing bully boy, recruited thousands of ex-soldiers and members of the paramilitary Freikorps to form the Nazi Stormtroopers (*Sturmabteilungen* – **the SA**), a private army, which grew into a fearsome street fighting force. Röhm replaced Mayr as Hitler's chief link with the local army command, and provided useful contacts for the Nazi Party within the army and among like-minded 'patriotic associations'; Herman Goering, a highly decorated fighter pilot, was also useful in introducing Hitler to many important figures in Bavarian high society. Another important early recruit to the Nazi cause was Rudolf Hess, who had been awarded the Iron Cross First Class, and became Hitler's personal secretary. Indeed, so many ex-soldiers were involved in the Nazi Party, or more likely, were encouraged to become involved by their army superiors, it was more like an army propaganda unit, supported by a paramilitary private army, than a conventional political party.

Sturmabteilungen (SA): The Stormtroopers or 'Brownshirts', founded in 1921 as the private army of the Nazi Party, led by Ernst Röhm. Hitler viewed the SA as useful bully boys, but he did not feel they were an integral part of his racial elite and he refused to support the idea the SA would play a leading role within the armed forces of the Third Reich.

With a band of loyal supporters around him, Hitler pressed for the 'committee based' structure, supported by the 'old guard' in the party, to be replaced by a command structure in which a single leader would have complete control over party decision-making. Under this proposal, any party member wanting to challenge the leader's views, or alter the party programme, faced immediate expulsion [**Doc. 5, p. 114**]. At the first 'national congress' of the Nazi Party, held in Munich, on 21 January 1921, Drexler claimed Hitler's desire for a strong leadership of the party was really a disguised bid for the leadership of the party and the proposal to change the structure of the party was rejected.

In the spring of 1921, Drexler, in a move designed to weaken Hitler's stranglehold over the party, held secret talks with the German Socialist Party (*Deutsch-Sozialistische* Party – DDP), founded by Alfred Brunner, an engineer from Dusseldorf, concerning a possible merger of the two nationalist parties. These negotiations went as far as agreeing the headquarters of the merged party, designated for Berlin – not Munich. Not surprisingly, Hitler was strongly opposed to the merger plans, which, if implemented, would have threatened his supremacy over the tightly knit Munich-based Nazi Party. Instead of attempting to win the argument through discussion, Hitler, took the prima donna option, and threw a temper tantrum. On 11 July 1920, Hitler – totally unwilling to compromise – resigned from the Nazi Party. The initial response of the party committee to Hitler's resignation was to publish a pamphlet, accusing Hitler of wanting to become a 'party dictator', criticising his 'bohemian' way of life, and even suggesting (unbelievably) that Hitler was in 'the pay of the Jews'. In response, Hitler set out his own uncompromising personal terms for rejoining the party: he wanted to be elected as 'party chairman', with 'dictatorial powers'. Drexler and the other members of the committee, soon realising the loss of its star speaker was a potentially mortal blow to the party, and fearing he might establish a popular rival party of his own, decided to accede to Hitler's demands. At a specially convened 'national congress' of the Nazi Party, which opened on 29 July 1921, the proposal that Hitler be given 'dictatorial' control over the party was carried by 553 to one.

THE GROWTH OF THE 'FÜHRER CULT'

In a very short space of time, Hitler had taken complete control of the Nazi party. He quickly attempted to bring local branches of the party, outside of the Munich area, under his control by issuing them with 'directives'. At first, local party activists, accustomed to having discussions on issues and passing resolutions, disregarded Hitler's orders. But they soon relented. In January 1922, for example, Hitler won a massive vote of confidence from the party membership for a proposal for all branches of the party to be subordinate to the personal will of the leader and directives from the central party head-quarters in Munich. As Hitler's power over the party increased, all semblance of autonomy previously enjoyed by local branches disappeared. At the end of 1922, Hitler created the post of delegate in charge of a local branch of the party, who was expected to ensure the decisions of the leader were enacted at the local level.

Under Hitler's leadership, the Nazi Party – from 1921 to 1923 – became the most vocal supporter of the idea of overthrowing the democratic Weimar Republic by force. To further this aim, Hitler enhanced the status and role of the SA under the leadership of Ernst Röhm. Previously, the SA was little more than a rowdy mob of bouncers whose main role was to keep order at Nazi party meetings. After Hitler took complete charge of the Nazi Party, the SA was turned into a loud and raging paramilitary force, ready and willing to 'rescue Germany'. Under Röhm's shrewd leadership, the SA improved its relations with the other paramilitary groups operating in the Munich region. Hence, the Nazi Party – under Hitler – operated not the politics of the ballot box, but the politics of the knuckleduster.

Throughout 1922, Hitler's speeches were consistently 'for Germany' and 'against' democratic government. Rumours also circulated which indicated Hitler was preparing to launch a 'putsch' in Munich, to be followed by a 'march on Berlin' to crush German democratic government. In October 1922, Hitler persuaded members of the DSP, a similar 'national-socialist'-style party, based in Franconia in northern Bavaria to join the Nazi Party, thus increasing party membership to 20,000. Hitler also had success in gaining sympathisers to the Nazi cause from several similar *Volkisch* groups in northern Germany, particularly in the Berlin area.

Mussolini's successful 'march on Rome' in October 1922, and the success-ful Fascist seizure of power in Italy which followed it, raised the spirits of nationalist groups in Germany. Before Mussolini seized power in Italy, Hitler always referred to himself in speeches as the 'drummer' of the revolt against democracy, not a future German 'dictator'. He gave the impression, especially to leading figures in the army and members of the Bavarian upper classes, that he would use his party and his speaking talent to serve the greater cause of a German counter-revolution against Weimar democracy in a subordinate role. After October 1922, however, Hitler started to believe he might be the 'dynamic leader' needed to lead Germany out of the perceived mire. Significantly, Nazi propaganda began to develop the cult of Hitler as 'Germany's Mussolini'. The comparison between the 'leaderless democracy' of the Weimar Republic and a Germany led by a 'great leader', determined to restore German pride and power, now became a central feature of Nazi propaganda. In December 1922, the *Völkischer Beobachter*, which had not previously depicted Hitler as a future German leader, now started, little by little, to suggest Hitler was the 'heroic' leader Germany needed.

THE MUNICH BEER HALL PUTSCH

During 1923, Hitler's speeches, which reached larger and larger audiences, emphasised the need for a 'strong man to rescue Germany'. Most Nazis – supported by the other nationalist groups – convinced themselves an armed insurrection in Bavaria could lead towards the toppling of the Weimar Republic. The major consequence of these ideas was the Munich Beer Hall Putsch of November 1923, a bungled attempt, led by Adolf Hitler to lead a 'march to Berlin', with the aim of toppling Weimar democracy.

The Munich Beer Hall Putsch grew out of a broad-based Bavarian nationalist conspiracy, which emerged during the crisis year of 1923 when hyperinflation brought Germany to the verge of economic collapse, and French troops occupied the industrial Ruhr in a futile attempt to extract reparations payments from the German government. These events created a tangible atmosphere of crisis that put great strain on the existing democratic order. Most of the democratic parties, supported by the majority of nationalists took part in the 'passive resistance' against the French occupation of the Ruhr. In a surprising move, Hitler opposed the policy of passive resistance, out of fear that opposition to France might encourage unity towards the existing German democratic government. 'Not down with France', Hitler said in a speech during the crisis, 'but down with the traitors to the Fatherland, down with the November criminals: that must be our slogan' (Fest, 1974: 164). Hitler's decision not to oppose the French occupation of the Ruhr prompted one leading Munich newspaper editorial to suggest the Nazi leader 'no longer captures the imagination of the German people' (Fest, 1974: 171). It is, indeed, hard to fathom why Hitler, always attentive to the popular nationalist mood, chose to take a stand that was so out of step with the popular mood. It seems Hitler, keen to topple Weimar democracy, was reluctant to throw his weight behind any cause that would strengthen it.

Meanwhile, the conspiracy to topple the Weimar Republic gathered momentum and supporters throughout Bavaria. Giving support to the conspiracy were: Hitler and the Nazi Party; leading figures within the local Bavarian command of the army (**Reichswehr**); the *Kampfbund*, a paramilitary militant association; some well-known 'Great War' military heroes, most notably General Ludendorff; and some prominent figures in the local police force, the Bavarian parliament, and an assortment of people in business and the local aristocracy. Taken as a whole, it was a powerful coalition of right-wing forces in Bavaria, provided they all stood together. In August

Reichswehr: The name of the Defensive Land Army created under the Weimar Republic (in 1935, it was renamed the Wehrmacht). The army played a very shady role during the Weimar period and was keen to support Hitler's rise to power, as many Generals were anti-communist and saw the Nazis as allies in dealing with the communist threat and likely to support increased spending on the armed forces.

1923, a plan to overthrow the republic had begun to take concrete shape. The aim was to overthrow the Weimar republican government, and to establish an authoritarian nationalist regime which would allow Bavaria complete autonomy. Stores of weapons, munitions and transport vehicles were collected together in preparation for what was seen as an inevitable showdown with central government. Following a pre-arranged signal from the leaders of the Bavarian government, a strong force of heavily armed conspirators, including units from the army, the *Kampfbund* and the leaders of far-right groups, with Hitler in the vanguard, would march north to the German capital with the aim of seizing power. The conspiracy was given fresh impetus on 26 September 1923 when Gustav von Kahr, a firm supporter of the conspiracy, was appointed as 'state commissioner' in Bavaria with 'dictatorial powers'. In this role, Kahr put Bavaria on a collision course with the Berlin government by refusing to proclaim a 'state of emergency' as he was requested to do by President Ebert under Article 48 of the Weimar constitution, and then by turning down a government request to ban the *Völkischer Beobachter*.

At the end of October 1923, the tactical details of the Bavarian conspiracy plan to overthrow the government were finalised by Kahr and his co-conspirators. In the early days of November 1923, however, some of the leading conspirators in the Bavarian government and the army started to have second thoughts, primarily because key figures in the army high command in Berlin told the Bavarian army conspirators they would defend the elected German government. On 3 November, General Otto von Lossow, the commander of the German army in Munich advised Kahr that any march on Berlin would be futile. On 6 November, Kahr told representatives of the leading paramilitary organisations that the Bavarian government, the army and the police would not support independent action designed to bring down the state. After hearing this, Hitler sought a meeting with Kahr, who refused to meet with him.

Hitler had staked his whole political career on the conspiracy going ahead. The trigger-happy right-wing paramilitary groups, whose support Hitler had assiduously nurtured for most of the year wanted action. In the end, Hitler, unclear about whether Kahr would go ahead or not, decided abandoning the project so late in the day would be a humiliation from which his own political reputation was unlikely to recover. So he decided to press on with what now seemed a hopeless enterprise.

On 8 November, Kahr was due to address an audience of prominent Munich government officials, and businessmen in a large Beer Hall (the *Bürgerbraukeller*) in the centre of Munich. Hitler suspected – quite wrongly – that Kahr intended to use the occasion to announce his own 'march on Berlin'. In fact, Kahr, and his supporters had already abandoned the whole project, and kept Hitler in the dark about their decision. At 8.30 pm Hitler, accompanied by armed SA men, entered the *Bürgerbraukeller*, while Kahr was in the midst of his speech. He jumped on a chair or a table (according to whose account you believe), then fired a single bullet from his revolver into the ceiling. Hitler then walked towards the platform and announced: 'The National Revolution has begun'; and that a new 'provisional' Reich government had been formed [**Doc. 6, p. 114**]. Of course, this was a very big lie: all Hitler had captured – and not for very long – was a large Munich Beer Hall. Kahr was led, at pistol point by Hitler, accompanied by Colonel Hans von Seisser, head of the Bavarian state police, and Lossow towards a small anteroom to discuss the 'national revolution'. Kahr found it difficult to take the whole matter seriously. Hitler offered him the post of regent of Bavaria, but the experienced local politician replied: 'Herr Hitler, you can have me shot or shoot me yourself. Whether I die is of no matter' (Shirer, 1961: 96). Hitler – beginning to realise that everything was not going according to plan – asked an SA man to go and collect General Ludendorff by car and bring him to the Beer Hall in the hope his exalted presence might encourage Kahr to change his mind. When Ludendorff did arrive, about half an hour later, he told Kahr he supported Hitler. This appears to have impressed Kahr to some extent. However, Ludendorff was surprised to learn from the Nazi leader that in the 'new' and fictional German government he had been assigned the post of commander of the army, and Hitler had appointed himself as the 'dictator of Germany'.

What happened next on this farcical evening is a matter of some dispute. Hitler claimed – at his later trial – that Kahr, Seisser and Lossow all agreed to join the conspiracy. Some of those present on the evening stated that Kahr did return to the platform, after speaking with Hitler and Ludendorff, and announced he would support 'Hitler's Putsch' [**Doc. 6, p. 114**]. It seems Kahr only did this because he was forced to at gunpoint. Kahr, Seisser and Lossow later said they all intended to suppress the revolt, as soon as they were free to do so. What they did not say, of course, was that they had been plotting a conspiracy against the Berlin government themselves for many months and had only abandoned the project at the eleventh hour. Ludendorff claimed he knew nothing of what Hitler intended to do at the Beer Hall – and was taken by surprise by Hitler's impetuous action. Of course, he also omitted to say he had been conspiring with Hitler for months.

Hitler finally left the Beer Hall at 10.30 am to go and calm down a clash between an SA paramilitary unit and troops which had erupted at the local barracks of the Army Engineers' a few miles away. Once Hitler departed, so did Kahr, Seisser and Lossow. Kahr quickly took measures to strangle the rebellion at birth. He moved the Bavarian government to Regensburg, then issued a proclamation, flyposted by the police throughout the Munich area, which claimed his earlier support for Hitler had been given at gunpoint. At the same time, he announced that the Nazi Party and the paramilitary *Kampfbund* were now banned organisations. In the meantime, the Nazis had not taken control of a single army barracks or any important government building.

A few minutes before midnight, Hitler accepted his attempt to overthrow Weimar democracy had failed miserably, primarily because his supposed partners in the enterprise were not willing to support him. During the night, Hitler appeared totally clueless as to what to do next. After all, he had planned a putsch against the despised Berlin government, not his right-wing friends in the Bavarian government and his former paymasters in the local army. As a final gesture, he agreed – after some persuasion – to lead a demonstration through Munich (which took place on 9 November) in the vague hope this show of strength would miraculously rouse the army belatedly to support a 'march to Berlin'. 'If it comes off, all's well', Hitler told a close confidante, 'if not, we'll hang ourselves' (Fest, 1974: 187). Hitler led the demonstration, wearing his trademark shabby raincoat, along with the hapless Ludendorff, who had remained loyal to him, and a group of about 2,000 Nazis (including 300 armed SA men). The group intended to march to the War Ministry building and seize it. But, as they reached a street, leading to the Odeonplatz, the marchers found the route blocked by an armed police cordon. Several shots were then fired by both sides. At the end of this exchange, lasting less than two minutes, fourteen members of the Nazi group, and four policemen were dead, while others lay wounded. In the middle of the mayhem, Hitler fell awkwardly to the ground, dislocating his shoulder on landing. After getting to his feet, he ran away from the scene, leaving the dead and dying behind, and escaped in an ambulance. He later claimed – rather unconvincingly – that he had left so quickly because he thought Ludendorff had been killed, which was surely a reason for him to stay. Some years later, he concocted another story – also untrue – that he had bravely carried a child away from the scene to a waiting ambulance. In reality, Hitler's nerve failed him at the vital moment. When it was all over, Hitler turned up at the Munich house of a close friend: Ernst 'Putzi' Hanfstangl, a local wealthy landowner, where he was arrested by the police, and taken to Landsberg prison on 11 November, to await trial on a charge of treason.

The Munich Beer Hall Putsch – the most significant event in the early history of the Nazi Party was a hurriedly planned, bungled, and humiliating failure. It failed because Hitler had allowed the Nazi Party to become a paramilitary organisation during 1923, and to become subsumed inside a conspiracy, involving many disparate elements of the Bavarian right over which he had no control, and precious little significant influence. Although Hitler has been viewed as the instigator of the conspiracy to overthrow the German state in 1923, the reality was very different. It was really the Bavarian 'right', composed of the Bavarian government, the local army command and the state police which had flirted with the idea of a 'Putsch' against the Berlin government, and it was they who decided – very late in the day – to abandon the project, once they realised it had no support from the army high command in Berlin. Hitler – who had never been taken into the heart of the conspiracy – had meanwhile whipped up his own supporters into a frenzy, only to find he had already been deserted by his co-conspirators before he ever arrived at the *Bürgerbraukeller*. To make matters worse, they did not consider him important enough to even inform him of their change of heart. Hitler felt he could not retreat without damaging his own claim to be the leading 'revolutionary' against Weimar democracy – so he pressed on towards humiliating failure. In the early days of November 1923, therefore, it seemed Adolf Hitler's brief but extremely colourful political career had come to an abrupt and untimely end.

4

The Ideology of Hitler and the Nazi Party

Nazism was a vague 'eclectic ragbag ideology' which drew on a wide variety of sources. It lacked the coherent, and systematic economic foundations of Marxist-Leninist communism. It is even difficult to determine whether it was 'progressive' or 'backward looking'. Unlike Marxism, which aimed to destroy the existing economic and political system, Nazism was much more willing to collaborate with existing power structures, and to follow seemingly backward-looking ideas in pursuit of its objectives. Nazism also lacked the ideological backing and intellectual weight of a Karl Marx. In essence, Nazism was a rather ill-thought-out 'third way' between liberal democracy and communism. It grew at a time when mass democracy was being introduced in Germany for the first time and when the world economic system was greatly strained by the consequences of First World War.

Nazism built its support by tapping into the negative feelings of certain sections of German society towards such things as the 'harsh' terms of the Versailles Treaty, high inflation, the instability of democratic government, the economic position of Jews in German society and the growth of a vibrant communist movement. Nazi ideology pointed to the 'enemies' inside Germany: communists, socialists, trade unionists, democrats and Jews, and then suggested the elimination of these groups from positions of power could only be achieved through a 'National Socialist Revolution' that would establish a strong state, led by a strong leader, determined to re-build military power, shake off Versailles and make Germany, once and for all, the most dominant power in the world.

LINKS WITH FASCISM AND TOTALITARIANISM

Although Nazism had many unique characteristics, there has always been a tendency to bracket it under the general label of 'fascism', a term which

invokes words such as 'violent', 'repressive' and 'dictatorial'. However, finding a general theory of 'fascism' has proved extremely difficult. For a start,
there was no great philosopher who codified fascist ideology. This is hardly
surprising as fascism prided itself on being anti-intellectual and opposed
to 'rational' thought. It is not surprising, therefore, to discover that the statements and writings of the leading supporters of fascism are as dense as
fog [**Doc. 8, p. 116**]. The incoherence and anti-intellectual nature of fascism
reflected the narrowness of the minds who supported it. The only explanation Mussolini, the Italian fascist leader, ever offered for the ideological basis
of fascism was a short article, published in an Italian encyclopedia, in which
he defined a fascist as a fervent patriot for whom the preservation of the state
is most crucial. To Marxists, the strident uncritical patriotic loyalty fascists
expressed towards a powerful state was merely a 'bourgeois device' used by
upper-class reactionary groups, who wanted to crush mass democracy, communism and the growing labour movement in one fell swoop in order to
safeguard their own threatened position at the top of society. This view is
reinforced by the fact that authoritarian dictatorships in Germany and Italy
were established through the existing legal and administrative machinery
of these states, and supported by many upper-class elite groups in the army,
civil service and big business. A more sophisticated version of the idea of
fascism being a sort of 'elite conspiracy' to crush communism and democracy
was offered by the leading Italian Marxist writer Antonio Gramsci (who was
executed by the Fascists). He suggested that capitalism – especially in Europe
– was going through a severe crisis in the early part of the twentieth century,
in which the dominant classes of the nineteenth century were finding it
increasingly difficult to manipulate the mass of the population to support their
rule, and were concerned that communism might sweep them away in a tidal
wave of revolution. In these circumstances, fascism became the repressive
means of restoring their hegemony over society by offering the masses a
seemingly popular form of rule led by a dominant individual, when in reality
it was merely a vehicle for destroying the threatening power of communism
and the egalitarian principles of mass democracy. Of course, the problem with
this view of fascism is that it attaches very little importance to the popularity
of fascism among certain sections of German and Italian society, which, on
this view, was manipulated.

Seymour Lipset, in his influential study, *Political Man*, viewed fascism in
a rather different way, portraying it as a genuine 'revolt of the middle classes'
who felt trapped between the growth of big business and the revolutionary
politics of the workers and thought the liberal democratic parties could not
haul them out of the mounting economic distress after 1918 or restore the
stability and order they so desired. On this view, fascism had a genuine mass
appeal to these groups and was not simply imposed upon them from above

through manipulation (Payne, 1995: 349). However, Lipset's interpretation, which concentrated on the German case alone, has been challenged by many studies of voting behaviour in Germany from 1918 to 1933, which have shown that the Nazi Party did not just gain votes from disaffected liberals, but drew the bulk of its support from small right-wing nationalist fringe parties, from prosperous members of the upper middle class, and from a significant number of voters in rural areas who had previously not voted for any other party.

The problem of finding a general theory to explain 'fascism' is further complicated by the development of the concept of 'totalitarianism' which argues that communist and fascist dictatorships in power were different sides of the same coin. Carl Friedrich, for example, put forward a 'six point' test to evaluate a 'totalitarian' regime, consisting of: an official ideology, a single mass party, a terrorist police force, monopoly control of the media, a monopoly of arms, and central control of the economy. Totalitarian regimes of the communist or fascist variety made the masses conform to their rule or face dire consequences. The main problem of the totalitarian model is that it is a rather static model, which views communist and fascist regimes as basically similar, thus downplaying the actual ideological differences and aims of Nazism in Germany and Bolshevism in the Soviet Union and by especially failing to see the real economic differences and class relationships within each society.

The acceptance of a general theory of fascism has also encountered similar problems of gaining credibility among historians and political scientists. No single theory of fascism can possibly explain the different characteristics of the many different regimes and political parties which called themselves 'fascist' and operated throughout Europe during the inter-war period. Even Nazism and Italian Fascism exhibited major ideological differences. Race was of fundamental significance in Nazi ideology, but of comparative insignificance to Italian Fascists. Mussolini gave open support to many aspects of modernity, while Hitler tended to stress the need to incorporate many lost medieval customs into German society. At the same time, there were many similarities between Italian Fascism and National Socialism, including, extreme nationalism, emphasis on strong dictatorial leadership, a strong anti-Marxism, which implied the destruction of working-class and Marxist organisations, ruthless repression of all opposition groups, contempt for democratic forms of government, the glorification of war, strong support for rearmament, a stress on the need for economic self-sufficiency, the use of propaganda and, especially, in the rise to power of Mussolini and Hitler, the forging of alliances with existing anti-democratic elites within the state, and the creation of paramilitary organisations of ex-soldiers to add to the sense of general chaos on the streets. In most respects, fascist ideology opposed existing 'established' religion, but at the same time projected a messianic mission, which resembled a devotion to a religious faith. Fascism was a sort of political religion, which expressed a rather utopian vision of the future, in which a new state and a 'new man' would prosper. Fascism also stressed action and daring, which appealed to young people. Another key characteristic of fascist ideology was its stress on male chauvinism and male domination over society. Fascist ideology had little interest in women's equality or women's rights.

In spite of the similarities between the Italian and German versions of fascism, many historians do not accept Nazism was simply a mere derivative version of Italian Fascism, primarily because the specific differences between Italian Fascism and National Socialism when examined in detail outweigh the similarities, especially, the over-arching race theory within National Socialism, to which all other aspects of Nazi ideology and policy were inextricably linked. Put this way, Nazism can be viewed as a unique phenomenon because its emphasis on race, and the anti-modern idea of the *Volkisch* state differed greatly from the modernist ideas of Italian Fascism. More importantly, Hitler's unique personality and ideological obsession with race gave Nazism specific German–Austrian characteristics which must be analysed in the context of the historical development of Germany.

THE HISTORICAL ROOTS OF NAZISM

No major historical force emerges without some prior development and the historical roots of Nazism stretched back into history. Nazi propaganda certainly acknowledged its debt to many past historical influences. Hitler claimed 'A man who has no sense of history, is like a man who has no eyes and ears' (Bullock, 1962: 397). A famous Nazi postcard, very popular in the Nazi period, featured Hitler's head alongside those of Frederick the Great, Bismarck and Hindenburg. Hitler frequently claimed Nazi rule represented a continuity as the Third Reich, with the First Reich (the medieval Holy Roman Empire), and the Second Reich (established by Bismarck – and ended by the 1919 peace settlement). Even in his bunker, up until his suicide, Hitler kept a portrait of Frederick the Great, the eighteenth-century soldier-King, on a bedside table.

Some historians have suggested that Germany followed a special and unique historical path (*Sonderweg*), which glorified authoritarian rule, war and territorial conquest. National Socialism was a logical consequence of these German preoccupations. Many of Hitler's supposedly 'unique' foreign policy aims turn out, on closer inspection, not to have been so novel after all. The concept of **Lebensraum**, the acquisition of living space, not only had historical precedents in German history, but was mentioned frequently in

Lebensraum: Living space. A key concept in Hitler's foreign policy thinking. The idea was for the German armed forces not only to defeat the enemy but also to de-populate areas captured and use them to expand Germans on to the newly acquired land.

most of the pre-1914 Pan-German League pamphlets. German dominance of eastern Europe and the subordination of the Slavs were key aims, not only of Frederick the Great in the eighteenth century but also of the Kaiser during the First World War. Most conservative nationalist groups in Germany – even in the Weimar period – advocated most of Hitler's foreign policy aims. On the other hand, many other historians have suggested Nazism had no deep roots in German history. Nationalism, anti-Semitism and social Darwinism, all regarded as key influences on Nazism, were actually ideas imported from outside Germany. A policy of systematic killing – aimed at the Jewish population – had no precedent in pre-1914 German policy.

It is, in fact, possible to view Nazism as a unique German response to specific problems thrown up by the First World War: a reaction against modern and urbanised industrial society; a reaction against rapid techno-logical change and innovation; a reaction against the growth of socialism and mass democracy; a response to the development of mass society; a response to deep economic problems – most notably – high inflation; and a desire to restore confidence in a defeated nation. It is very difficult to isolate the long-term historical influences on the development of Nazism from the particular characteristics of the period in which it gained prominence.

THE PHILOSOPHICAL ROOTS OF NATIONAL SOCIALISM

Attempting to isolate the philosophical roots of National Socialism are equally complex. A great deal of ink has been spilled trying to explain where Hitler got his ideas from. Hitler, although he was an avid reader, did not read philosophical tracts in depth, and regarding him as some sort of ideological guru is quite absurd. Many of Hitler's ideas – especially in the period after the First World War – were shared by some of the leading members of the Nazi Party. One important figure who influenced Hitler in the early days of the Nazi Party in Munich was Dietrich Eckart, a poet, playwright and journalist, whose best friend was a wine glass. Hitler described Eckart – a serious alcoholic – as 'a fatherly friend'. He claimed to have been greatly influenced by Eckart's second-hand nationalist and anti-Semitic ideas. Eckart was very fond of telling his fellow Nazi members to 'keep your blood pure', even though his own blood was always somewhat heavily diluted by alcohol. Eckart was the author of several early Nazi pamphlets from which Hitler undoubtedly drew inspiration, including a bitter attack on 'The Jews' entitled: 'That is the Jew', which argues the restoration of the German **Volk** could only be achieved through the 'removal of the Jewish menace' (Zalampas, 1989: 37). Eckart's virulent anti-Semitism, and his flaky eugenic theories concerning race were

Volk: Race. A central concept in Nazi ideology. Indeed, recent studies are showing just how integral racial ideas were within the Nazi elite.

a very profound influence on Hitler's own ideas on these subjects. It seems that word-of-mouth ideas, received second-hand, exerted a greater impact on Hitler's ideas than any deep reading of philosophy.

While in Landsberg fortress, Hitler claimed he read works by Nietzsche, Hegel, Houston Stewart Chamberlain and Treitschke, even though those present at the time later claimed he rarely read such works in any detail. Nevertheless, it is possible to detect Hegel's view of the state having 'supreme power over the individual' in Hitler's writings and speeches. Heinrich von Treitschke, the German historian, did influence Hitler, in particular, his view that 'war was the highest expression of man'. There is also little doubt that the work of Nietzsche, however assimilated, penetrated into Hitler's thinking. Nietzsche was a German philosopher who was deeply disturbed by the dizzy pace of European social and industrial change. He predicted modern society would result in 'the death of God'. What Hitler latched on to in Nietzsche's writings were his fervent criticisms of democratic forms of government, his praise of violence and war, and his prediction of the emergence of the coming 'master race' led by an all-powerful 'superman', supported by a small elite, which together would 'rule the world'. The term 'Lords of the Earth' coined by Nietzsche, is constantly expressed throughout *Mein Kampf*, and was repeatedly mentioned by Hitler – and most of the leading Nazis – during the era of the Third Reich. Neitszche was certainly treated as a deep philosophical influence on National Socialism during the Nazi era, even if the nuances of his philosophy were way beyond the bar-room logic of most Nazis. There is equally little doubt that Hitler viewed himself as a 'superman', who had been marked out by 'providence' to lead Germany to the pinnacle of world power.

Hitler was very clearly attracted by the idea of the 'survival of the fittest', and a crude social Darwinism permeates a great deal of his writings and speeches. By the late nineteenth century, and in the early twentieth century, social Darwinistic ideas, derived largely from anthropological and zoological research, were extremely fashionable in Germany and Austria, and through-out most of western Europe. Such theories tended to reinforce the appeal of nationalism, especially in Germany and Austria. Hitler did believe life was a 'struggle between strength and weakness' in which only the strong would prevail, through the use of superior force. Although such ideas were influenced by the writings of Charles Darwin, there is no evidence Hitler ever read any of his work in the original. Even so, Hitler was unquestionably a social Darwinist, and this was a key ideological influence upon his ideas.

Closely related to social Darwinist thinking were ideas about race, which was another dominant aspect of Nazi ideology. Modern racial concepts of discriminatory racism were postulated during the eighteenth-century Enlightenment in the writings of leading European geographers and anthropologists, but they grew more well-known from the mid-nineteenth century. The thinker whose work greatly influenced future writers on race was Compte Arthur de Gobineau who divided humanity into three basic races – white, yellow and black – and who put forward the view that race was the key to the development of history. Gobineau argued that all higher forms of civilisation had flowed from the superior 'white race', and the highest form of that race was the 'Aryan': the highest human species of all. According to Gobineau, the purity of the Aryan race had decayed over centuries due to racial mixing 'with inferior races'. The only means of creating a future master race, according to Gobineau, was to ensure that 'Aryans' only produced children in union with other Aryans. Yet he was pessimistic about whether this could ever be achieved.

Other racial theorists rejected the pessimism in Gobineau's writings and called instead for eugenic policies to defend the so-called 'higher races'. Such ideas on race soon became popular in many parts of Europe and were particularly extensive throughout German-speaking central Europe. The greatest populariser of racist ideas in Germany and Austria was an eccentric Englishman who had settled in Germany: Houston Stewart Chamberlain, who was a leading figure in the German branch of the Gobineau Society. It was Chamberlain who popularised Gobineau's theories on race in his famous book, *Foundations of the Nineteenth Century* (1899), which became extremely popular with Pan-German groups in Germany, and provided the Nazis with the basis of their master race ideas. Chamberlain popularised the idea in Germany and Austria that the key driving force in historical development was race. At the top of the racial pyramid was the 'Teuton' ('the soul of our culture'), whose highest form was the 'tall, blond, blue-eyed, magnificent'. Aryan found in its 'purest form' in Germany. It was through the development of the Aryan that Germans could become the 'masters of the earth'. The ultimate anti-Aryan and most 'bitter racial foe' was 'the Jew'. There is little doubt that in Germany and Austria, the rapid growth in popularity of racial doctrines which eulogised the 'Aryan' were always accompanied by anti-Semitism.

Another important influence on Hitler's ideas were the musical operatic works, and political views of Richard Wagner. Hitler often claimed that anyone wanting to understand fully National Socialism 'must know Wagner'. Wagner harboured a strong dislike of 'the Jews', and he venerated German nationalism in many of his operas (Shirer, 1961: 133). What particularly attracted Hitler to Wagner were his vividly staged operas, which pitted German medieval heroes, with tribal codes in a struggle against their enemies. In a very real sense, Nazism was not just about ideas, but was really about putting ideas into action. Hitler viewed Nazi Germany as the enactment of some great real-life theatrical opera, and the vast Nazi displays of pomp and ceremony, which characterised so much of the ceremonial life of the Nazi Party, owed a great deal to the inspiration of the operas of Wagner. Indeed, the end of *Goetterdaemerung*, when Wotan, the leading character, sets on fire Valhalla has great similarities to Hitler's flame-filled hell in Berlin at the end of the Second World War.

What these ideas on race tended to reinforce was a strong form of defensive nationalism. There is little doubt that the intense feelings of nationalism that existed in Germany, Austria and among the upper classes throughout European society in the early part of the twentieth century were linked to fears about the consequences of the growth of internationalism, and especially the growing popularity of the anti-nationalist creed of Marxism. Though right-wing nationalist groups did not appeal for support to nationalism alone, it was a key aspect of their ideological thinking. Hence, Nazism can be viewed as a reactionary response to the growth of socialist forces, and the growth of mass democracy, and modern urban industrial society. Nazism sought to recapture the revolutionary potential of nationalism, which had first come to prominence during the era of the French Revolution.

HITLER'S CENTRAL ROLE IN NAZI IDEOLOGY

Of course, the key to understanding the essence of Nazism does not lie only in isolating the various influences on National Socialism, but in grasping how these ideas were assimilated into Nazi ideology by Adolf Hitler. The major source for comprehending Nazi ideology is *Mein Kampf* (*My Struggle*), written by Hitler, and published in two volumes (the first volume appeared in July 1925, the second in December 1926). The original title: 'Four and a Half Years of Battle Against Lies, Stupidity and Cowardice: Account Settled' was rejected as too long-winded by Max Amann, Hitler's publishing manager. *Mein Kampf* is part autobiography, part ideological tract, and part blueprint for political action. It is not a great work of political theory, running to 752 pages – in its original form – of verbose, subjective and repetitive prose which reads like the extended ranting of an extremely prejudiced person. In spite of these obvious weaknesses, *Mein Kampf* remains a very important book for understanding the essence of Nazi ideology because it outlines the most complete presentation of the fundamental principles of Hitler's *Weltanschauung* ('world view' – or ideology), the techniques of Nazi propaganda, the plan for destroying Marxism, and eliminating Jews from German society, the concept and policies of a future National Socialist state and Hitler's central foreign policy objectives. Between 1925 and 1945, *Mein Kampf* sold 10 million copies and was translated into sixteen languages. It made Hitler a very rich man and the world a poorer place.

THE IMPORTANCE OF FOREIGN POLICY

The central foreign policy aim of Nazism was to make Germany the most dominant power in Europe, and to gain revenge for the German defeat in the First World War. As a result, the largest amount of space in *Mein Kampf* is concerned with the aims of German foreign policy under Hitler's rule. Hitler's first objective was to 'abolish the Treaty of Versailles'. To achieve this, Hitler intended to revise the treaty by unilateral acts when suitable opportunities arose. If Hitler's foreign policy objectives had been merely limited to revising Versailles, the course of German history would have been very different, and Hitler would now be judged as one of the most successful German leaders in history. However, doing away with the 'hated' Versailles Treaty was for Hitler just the essential prelude to a resurgence of German militarism of a more extreme variety than had existed before. 'To demand that the 1914 frontiers of Germany be restored', wrote Hitler in *Mein Kampf*, 'is a political absurdity'. In fact, Hitler – although often accused of being a counter-revolutionary – was deeply critical of pre-1914 German foreign policy, especially the aim of seeking a colonial empire outside Europe – the so-called 'World Policy' – and engaging in a wasteful naval rivalry with Britain. Instead, Hitler intended to concentrate his own territorial aims exclusively on the European continent. To begin with, Hitler would incorporate all German speakers in Austria, the Sudetenland and Poland into a greater German Reich. Hitler knew these territorial acquisitions would meet opposition from the French government. Hence, a war with France – 'the inexorable enemy of the German people' – was always implicit in Hitler's foreign policy thinking. As a counterweight to French hostility to German aims in Europe, Hitler wanted to build close relations with Britain, thereby avoiding the severe Anglo-German antagonism which had characterised relations between the two countries in the years which led to the outbreak of the First World War. Indeed, Hitler hoped to persuade the British government to abandon its long-standing support for upholding a balance of power in Europe, and enter an alliance with Germany under whose terms the British empire would be guaranteed in return for Britain allowing Germany a 'free hand' to gain territory in eastern Europe without interference.

The major aim of Hitler's foreign policy – closely linked to his racial ideas – was to gain *Lebensraum* (living space) for Germany in eastern Europe through a war of conquest against the Soviet Union. According to Hitler: 'If land is desired in Europe, it could be obtained by and large only at the expense of the Soviet Union, and this meant the new Reich must set itself on the march along the road of the Teutonic Knights of old, to obtain by the German sword, sod for the German plough and daily bread for the nation.' The aim of *Lebensraum* was to defeat the Soviet Union in war, providing enough living space to assure German 'freedom of existence' and paving the way for a German population explosion in the newly acquired areas. The eventual aim was to create a Greater German Reich of two hundred and fifty million 'racially pure' Germans completely self-sufficient in food and raw materials. In Hitler's view, the task of gaining *Lebensraum* in the east had been made easier for the German army because of the Russian Revolution, which had 'handed over Russia to the Jews' and thereby weakened its military prowess. The war of conquest against the Soviet Union was, for Hitler, not only a clear and concrete aim, but also a crusade to rid eastern Europe of his two most hated enemies: Bolsheviks and Jews. Of course, the concept of *Lebensraum* did not originate with Hitler. It was a common term used by many groups on the right of German politics in the Weimar period. The idea was very strongly featured in pre-1914 Pan-German League pamphlets, many of which we know were read by Hitler during his Vienna period. It appears to have been used interchangeably by those right-wing groups which desired a unification of all 'German speakers' (**Volksdeutsche**) who were scattered throughout eastern Europe, and those groups (such as the Nazi Party) which used the concept to justify support for vast territorial conquest for Germany in eastern Europe, primarily at the expense of the Soviet Union. At the root of the concept was the idea of Germans not having enough land to live on, thereby reducing Germany's ability to become a dominant world power. The central aim of the future National Socialist state was to prepare the German people for a war of conquest in eastern Europe to gain *Lebensraum* at the expense of the Soviet Union.

Volksdeutsche: Ethnic Germans.

THE CENTRALITY OF RACE

The dominant theoretical factor in Nazi ideology was race. Hitler was not, as is often routinely argued, a mere 'German nationalist', as he often conceded – mostly in private – that the concept of the 'Aryan' race extended to many other people in central Europe, and even to England and to some 'Aryan' people throughout Europe and Anglo-Saxons in the USA. Such revolutionary ideas, which became more apparent during the Second World War, would have frightened many Germans, and weakened the appeal of Nazism before 1933, so Hitler kept quiet about them.

Hitler viewed all of human history, not as a class struggle, but as a struggle for existence between strong and pure races over weak and mixed ones. War ('that great purifier') was viewed by Hitler as the means through which the strongest and purest race would dominate the weak. The question as to how Germans will become the strongest race on earth occupies a great deal of Hitler's attention in *Mein Kampf*. Hitler divided the world into three racial groups: (i) 'Aryans' – defined as those races who created cultures (ii) the 'bearers of culture' – classed as those races who cannot create culture, but who can copy from Aryans (iii) 'inferior peoples' – defined as having no capacity to create culture, or copy from others, only capable of destroying cultures. The key objective of Hitler's racial policy, therefore, was to create a racially pure 'Aryan' folk community (**Volksgemeinschaft**) of Germans, which, due to its alleged 'superiority' gave it the right to subjugate 'inferior' people.

Volksgemeinschaft: The Folk Community. The Nazi slogan expressing the desire to create a classless unified German society.

THE FUNCTION OF ANTI-SEMITISM AND ANTI-MARXISM IN NAZI IDEOLOGY

If the 'Aryan' possessed all the positive qualities Hitler admired, the opposite was true of Hitler's two most hate-inspired enemies: Marxists and Jews. Hitler regarded the Marxist desire to foment a 'class war' as the chief threat to the unity of the nation. A virulent hatred of Marxism – and everything associated with it – runs through all of Hitler's writings and speeches [**Doc. 11, p. 118**]. At the core of Hitler's ideological mission, was a desire to 'eliminate' Marxism within Germany, and then to 'exterminate' Bolshevism during a war against the Soviet Union. At his trial for treason in March 1924, Hitler told the court he wanted to be 'the breaker of Marxism' and elsewhere he frequently spoke of his desire to 'annihilate' Marxism.

Hitler's anti-Marxism was interwoven with a virulent anti-Semitism. Whenever Hitler spoke of Marxists, he implied they were either 'Jews' or 'controlled by Jews'. Hitler defined 'the Jews' not as a religious group, but as a united race who were planning 'a world conspiracy' to undermine national unity. This far-fetched conspiracy was supposedly outlined in *The Protocols of Zion*, a forged document, which was circulated widely in Germany before 1914, and outlines a Zionist plan for Jewish world domination. Hitler believed that because Jews were a 'stateless people' (the state of Israel was not established until 1947), they sought to undermine the 'ethnic unity' and 'racial purity' of every state they inhabited. Hitler ascribed every ill in the world to 'Jewish influence'. Anti-Semitism had two functions within Nazi ideology: it provided a very simple explanation for all the divisions and problems in German society, and suggested a full solution to those ills could only be achieved by 'eliminating' Jews from German society. In Nazi ideology, 'the Jew' was a universal scapegoat, responsible for Marxism, democracy, internationalism, pacifism, class war, freedom of the press, prostitution, venereal disease, modernism in art, and much else. Behind every anti-patriotic disunifying force lay, according to Hitler, 'the eternal Jew', plotting and scheming to weaken the 'blood purity' and will of the Aryan race. Once again, the extreme radical nature of Hitler's anti-Semitism was toned down greatly, especially in the critical period from 1928 to 1933, as Nazi voting strength increased. In reality, Hitler's anti-Semitism was demonic in its passion and was a central aspect of his ideological thinking. Hitler never fully explained what he meant before 1933 about his desire to 'eliminate' the Jewish danger, but given his ideological mindset there is little doubt he saw such an elimination as 'extermination', if he got the chance, especially on a pan-European scale.

THE FOLK COMMUNITY

When Hitler discussed the future shape of the Nazi state, he thought in terms of creating a popular folk (or ethnically unified) community (*Volksgemeinschaft*), bound together by 'common blood' ties and guided by the will of an all-powerful leader. The idea of creating a folk community was a popular and nostalgic idea, supported by all sections of the German nationalist right. The German word '*Volk*' when translated into English is rendered usually as 'people' but in German it possessed a much deeper meaning, denoting an idealised return to a primitive rural form of ethnic unity based on 'blood and soil', with a romanticised (and often mythologised) view of Germany's medieval past and a strong belief that there was an ethnic and unique race – the Germans – with a shared set of values, deep bonds and blood ties stretching back in the lost mists of time. *Volkisch* nationalism tended to stress the unique and distinct aspects of 'German' people, culture and even the landscape. Most *Volkisch* writers claimed German medieval society was one in which tribes were bound together by shared language, feelings of loyalty, blood ties and love of working on the soil. The authority in such a society was passed down from a leader, who exercised power for the benefit of the whole community. The economy was based on self-sufficiency, home production, and fair barter between kith and kin in a romanticised folk community. When war came, so the *Volkisch* myth suggested, the whole community was united in a struggle for its own people. It was the creation of a modern industrial society which broke this unity by placing profits, productivity and trade above natural kindred bonds. Such attitudes tended to reject Christianity in favour of a mystical view of the past, the cosmos and the environment. Not surprisingly, the idea of the *Volk* tended to be opposed to industrialisation, individualism, urbanisation, class conflict and cosmopolitan ideas; a 'return to the soil' was idealised as the answer to these problems. The goal of supporters of these *Volkisch* ideals was a harmonious united society which idealised rural life.

The appeal of such ideas – in the pre-1914 period – was strongest among the lower-middle classes: traders and merchants, and small-scale farmers, but some elements in the landed aristocratic class who also felt threatened by the rapid growth of industrialisation, and the liberality of thought which accompanied it, were also attracted by these ideas. Not surprisingly, *Volkisch* groups felt all the 'modern' influences on German society were related to 'Jewish influence'. In pre-1914 German society, *Volkisch* groups were a very small minority group within the middle classes, with very limited representation in the Reichstag, usually in the form of small special-interest parties, with limited electoral support. What supporters of *Volkisch* ideas had lacked before 1914 was a major political party championing these romantic ideals.

In the aftermath of the German defeat in the First World War, however, support for this nostalgic and utopian vision of a 'lost Germany' gathered in strength and was certainly a factor which pervaded Nazi ideology and helped to attract support for the Nazi Party from the middle classes – and from the rural community. Most supporters of the *Volkisch* myth wanted a return to a simpler, less complicated, greener society, based on principles such as hierarchy, patriotism, social harmony, order and obedience. The idea of the urban dweller being trapped by modernity was a very strong image in Nazi propaganda, which elevated a love of nature, the landscape and working on the land as the real means to a happy and contented life [**Doc. 14, p. 121**]. The idea of creating a national community in which each individual would unite together in its service, led by a powerful leader, supported by an elite (similar to the old medieval Teutonic Knights) was at the centre of the Nazi appeal to the middle classes and to rural communities.

Hitler had a romanticised and utopian view of German culture, which he believed had been undermined by powerful 'non German' forces. In Hitler's view, the rural and racial harmony between knights and peasants of medieval times had been destroyed by the rise of the bourgeoisie, the growth of industrial society, the rise of socialism and the influence of 'the Jews' in German society. The way forward was, therefore, to take Germany backward, to a simpler rural lifestyle in which each German could live on the land. The type of government for such a folk community would be an authoritarian one, with no majority decisions, no democratic votes, one where everything was decided 'by one man' and an 'elite of leaders'. The leader would give orders downwards, which were expected to be obeyed. The individual in such a society was expected to follow orders, without question, or discussion. The future Nazi state would not promote equality, only equality of opportunity [**Doc. 10, p. 118**]. Yet the individual who prospered was expected to serve the 'common good', and be willing to be self-sacrificing in the service of the nation. Indeed, 'Common Good before Individual Good' was a key Nazi slogan. To the powerful *Volkisch* myth, Hitler added the idea of the front-line community (*Frontsgemeinschaft*), which consisted of the soldiers who had fought in a common struggle against the enemy in the First World War and who had been 'stabbed in the back' by socialists, war profiteers and Jews at home.

Plate 1 A clean and well-dressed Hitler (pictured at the centre of the back row) in a school photograph during his 4th form in Leonding.

Plate 2 A serious looking Hitler (circled) is pictured with a group of army colleagues during the First World War. The dog in the photo is Foxl, a stray Hitler adopted as his pet.

Plate 3 Hitler speaking at a nationalist meeting at Harzburg in the early 1930s. The man seated next to him (wearing horn-rimmed spectacles) is Alfred Hugenburg, the leader of the DNVP.

Plate 4 Hitler is pictured in front of a group of Stormtroopers at Gera in September 1931,shortly after the Nazi party had won power in the Thuringia local assembly.

Hitler attempted to suggest he would recreate the unity of the soldiers in the war into a German society under Nazi rule.

Hitler defined the folk community as a 'classless society' in which individuals would find their own 'natural level' through hard work, will-power and effort. Hitler did often speak of the entire German nation being of 'pure Aryan stock', but, on closer inspection, it is clear that Hitler felt it could be achieved by a process of selecting who should and should not have children in a Nazi-run society. The key aim was to rid all 'racial impurities' from German blood, thereby paving the way to a return to a *Volksgemeinschaft*, a 'blood pure' community of Germans, living in harmony on the land. Yet Hitler believed only an elite group ('based on the aristocratic idea of nature'), meaning stronger, taller, fitter and faster, would become part of the Aryan elite. Those who did not match up to the Aryan ideal of perfection would have to content themselves with being loyal and patriotic members of the folk community. The Nazi elite were the nobility (the Teutonic Knights), the remainder were loyal peasants and all were part of a united and contented folk community. In practice, Hitler was more pragmatic about *Volkisch* ideals than many of his followers. In his search for power, the anti-capitalist, anti-big-business and anti-bourgeois aspects of Nazi ideology were downplayed, and it was 'Jews and Marxists' who became the chief and easy targets of Nazi abuse. Attacking 'the Jews' was easier than attempting to dismantle modern industrial society and returning Germans to the land.

In essence, Nazism wanted to create the conditions in which there would be equality of opportunity, but Hitler did not favour an equal society [**Doc. 11, p. 118**]. It was possible to reach the top in Hitler's society, not just with traditional academic qualifications, but also with 'racial qualifications' which amounted to the ability to trace a long 'German' family tree, combined with the essential physical attributes of being blond, tall, fit and physically strong, while also including the abilities of the 'self made' businessman in this criteria. Hitler promised the Nazi state would promote the 'victory of the better and stronger', and demand the subordination of the 'inferior and the weaker'. German citizens were expected not to 'weaken' the 'purity of their blood' by having children with people of different races. If a racially pure, sort of thoroughbred elite of Germans could be created, then Hitler believed it would be 'the highest species of humanity on this earth'. When Hitler spoke of 'race' and 'purity of blood', therefore, he was always thinking of the creation of a 'racial elite' (**Herrenvolk**) who would rule society. All Germans could aspire to be part of the 'master race', but in reality, Hitler realised, only a small proportion of Germans would be able to meet his exacting restrictions on entry. Outside of the 'racial elite' in the proposed Nazi state were 'the masses'. Hitler spoke of 'nationalising the masses' through successful propaganda. He believed 'the masses' could be duped into supporting just about any policy:

Herrenvolk: Master race. The term was reserved for the supposed future 'racial elite' that would rule the Third Reich.

'If the same message was repeated over and over again'. In Hitler's view the great mass of people 'will more easily fall victim to a great lie than to a small one'. It seems clear 'the masses' had the same position as a private soldier in Hitler's mind: they were to follow orders, without comment. They were to support the policies of the Nazi elite – without comment. They were to accept the unequal nature of Nazi society – without comment. Nazism was, therefore, fundamentally a doctrine of equality of opportunity but one which accepted it was bolstering and strengthening a very hierarchical and unequal society.

THE FUNCTION OF SOCIALISM IN NATIONAL SOCIALISM

This helps to explain why Hitler was always extremely vague about where 'socialism' came into his proposed folk community. The issue of exactly what Hitler meant by 'National-Socialism', caused enormous divisions within the Nazi Party before 1933, and much confusion outside it [**Doc. 11, p. 118**]. Hitler claimed 'National-Socialism' was a 'dictatorship of the whole community'. It would aim to create a society in which there were no class barriers [**Doc. 12, p. 119**].

The idea of 'National-Socialism' had been an open topic of discussion among extreme German nationalists for many years before the advent of the Nazi Party. In the 1890s a Liberal pastor, Friedrich Naumann, set up a 'National-Social Association' which aimed to persuade industrial workers – who might be attracted to real socialism – to give support to the existing state. The terms 'German Socialism' and 'National Socialism' were used inter-changeably by members of anti-Marxist and anti-Semitic *Volkisch* groups in Germany and Austria. These groups attempted to stress that National Socialism was concerned with the strengthening of the nation, not narrow sectional interests.

Hitler favoured this concept of socialism, over the egalitarian variety espoused by 'real' socialists. Hitler defined his odd brand of 'socialism' in the following way: 'Whoever is prepared to make the national cause his own to such an extent that he knows no higher ideal than the welfare of his nation; whoever has understood our great national anthem, "*Deutschland über Alles*" to mean that nothing in the wide world surpasses in his eyes this Germany, people and land – that man is a socialist'. On this definition, National Socialism was a form of uncritical loyalty to the state. The 'radical' wing of the Nazi Party – led by Gregor Strasser – argued that a National Socialist state should control the economic life and resources of the nation, and then use them for the benefit of the whole community. Hitler realised such ideas would alienate business and army support. As a result, 'socialist' ideas were marginalised in the Nazi programme before Hitler came to power – and most of the supporters of these ideas were brutally killed in the blood purge (known as 'the Night of the Long Knives') which took place in 1933.

As we have seen, much of Nazi ideology was borrowed from ideas long current in nationalist and anti-Semitic groups, which were themselves borrowed from the ideas of right-wing philosophers and social Darwinist writers. Nazism, like a very large sponge, soaked up these ideas, and then wrung them out to form the misty sludge known as National Socialism. Yet the importance of ideology for Hitler, was not in the ideas themselves: most of them were mythologised and utopian dreams, unsuited to the practical realities of a modern industrial society, or were eugenic and racist mumbo-jumbo which, if applied, would inevitably lead, even though the road may be twisted, towards genocide and war. Hitler could scarcely define an 'Aryan', or a 'Jew', and he often admitted privately that most of his master race ideas had little chance of being achieved in his lifetime, if at all. What Nazi ideology could do successfully was to define – in exaggerated terms – internal enemies: 'the Jews and the Marxists' and external ones: France and the Soviet Union, which had to be 'destroyed' or 'eliminated' or 'exterminated' before the Germans could begin to create their *Volkisch* utopia. Yet in the period when Hitler rose to power, it was the optimistic and utopian dream of creating a harmonious *Volksgemeinschaft*, of racially pure Aryans which struck the most responsive chord among those people who decided to vote for the Nazi Party. Such a utopian dream could only have prospered in the dark of a very black night.

5

The Nazi Party: Organisation, Propaganda and Membership

The rapid growth in support for the Nazi Party is one of the most remarkable occurrences in political history. A great deal of credit for the rise of Nazism has been attributed to the leadership ability, hypnotic oratory and political flexibility of Adolf Hitler. But, the 'Hitler factor' alone cannot fully explain why the Nazi Party went from a small fringe party, based in Munich, to the most popular party in Germany between 1919 and 1932. In order to comprehend why the Nazis were able to mount a such a devastating challenge to the existing political order in Weimar Germany we must also examine three important aspects of the Nazi Party: organisation, propaganda and membership.

ORGANISATION

The Nazi Party had a centralised, hierarchical, but very efficient organisation, whose nerve centre was in Munich. The party was organised on the *Führerprinzip* (leadership principle), which held that the decisions of the leader were binding on every official, branch, and member of the party [**Doc. 5, p. 114**]. The leader ('**Führer**') of the party enjoyed dictatorial power over all the administrative and organisational functions of the party. He delegated power to individuals in return for complete loyalty to his leadership. Hitler had the right to hire and fire all the party's leading officials, and could even expel any individual party member. The leader also chose candidates at elections, and appointed all the leading officials of the party at national and local level. Hitler personally controlled – through his Munich office – the issuing of membership cards for each party member. The party rank and file – who dressed in brown shirts – were expected to take orders from the leader, and his selected Nazi elite, without discussion. 'I alone lead the movement' wrote Hitler in 1925, 'and no one can impose conditions on me so long as I personally bear

Führer: Leader (Adolf Hitler). Hitler was the undisputed leader of the Nazi Party and enjoyed total power over the decision making within the Nazi Party.

the responsibility' (Shirer, 1961: 151). In fact, no local Nazi leader had any legitimacy or authority without the support of the leader. At party conferences, Hitler discouraged delegates from putting forward new policies, and reserved the final decision on all resolutions put to the conference. This simple leadership structure – which had more in common with the army than a political party – had the benefit of being easily understood by all members, and helped keep disparate factions together at crucial points. Anyone who attempts to challenge or criticise Hitler's leadership was very quickly isolated, ostracised and forced to leave the party.

Yet the unique position of the party leader within the organisational structure does not fully explain how the Nazi party functioned at the grass roots level. There was a high level of disunity and instability within local branches of the Nazi Party. Hitler could not control every member on every issue. He had to devolve power from the centre to local Nazi regional leaders and local party organisations. This structure led to the creation of a number of regional leaders, and to a number of disputes between them, usually revolving around who was most loyally carrying out the 'Führer's will'. Yet these disputes between local regional leaders and party members tended to strengthen Hitler's leadership rather than weaken it, as it allowed him to play one group off against another.

The focal point of Nazi Party organisation was the central office of the party, based in Munich (from 1930 located at 'The Brown House'). The leader was supported in running the party by his private secretary (Rudolf Hess), who became the second most important party figure, because he opened, and often answered Hitler's mail, and acted as a key liaison figure between the party leader, and all other organisational groups within the party at national and local level. Hitler took all the major decisions, but he very often allowed Hess to make some important decisions on his behalf, and most of the routine ones. The other key figures at central office were: the chief organisational leader (Gregor Strasser), the executive secretary (Philipp Bouhler), the treasurer (Franz Schwarz), and the Propaganda Leader (Joseph Goebbels).

In the national organisation of the party, Gregor Strasser was the most powerful figure. As organisational leader, he directed the major activities of the party, and he was also in charge of nine other organisational 'Main Departments' located at central office, which were led by 'Shadow ministers' who formulated policies for the party. This highly centralised organisational structure allowed Strasser to regulate the activities of the party. In July 1932, Gregor Strasser headed a total staff at central office numbering 95 people, located in 54 separate offices. On the downside, increasing central control turned the Nazi Party – especially as its popularity and membership expanded – into a top-heavy bureaucracy. More full-time officials, and administrative staff, were employed by the Nazi Party in 1932 than in any other German political party. Hitler took pride in the fact that the Nazi Party ensured all party membership forms were filled out – and signed – at central office, in triplicate, with two copies kept on file, even though this process actually put more strain on the paperwork at central office. The great bulk of Nazi income by the early 1930s was used to pay the salaries of those who worked at central office, and to fund a growing army of paid functionaries at the local level. In practice, central office had to rely on local regional leaders, local party organisations, and a large network of ancillary organisations to ensure decisions made at the centre were implemented at the grass roots.

At the local level, the Nazi Party was divided into a large number of regional centres and local branches. Yet at every level of party organisation, the leadership principle operated. Each regional leader had authority over those beneath him (and they were all male) and took orders from whoever was above him in the party hierarchy. The country was divided for organisational purposes into 34 regional districts (**Gaue**), which corresponded roughly with the 34 Reichstag national electoral districts. At the centre of all local Nazi Party organisations was the regional leader of the party (the **Gauleiter**), who was not elected by local party activists, but directly appointed by the party leader, and subject to instant dismissal, if deemed not to be faithfully carrying out the 'Führer's will'. *Gauleiters* were 'local Führers', who were expected to carry out the 'Fundamental Directives' issued by the party leader. Although many local *Gauleiters* often pursued their own interests, the majority were loyal to the party leader. Each *Gauleiter* sent a monthly report to central office – on a specially printed form – which outlined the key activities and developments in his area. Each Gau was subdivided into a number of smaller '*Kreise* circles', chaired by a *Kreisleiter* (District Leader), each of whom was expected to carry out the orders of the *Gauleiter*. These orders were then transmitted down the chain of command to local branches, led by a 'Local Leader' and then transmitted further down the line to smaller 'Sections', 'Cells' and 'Tenement Blocks'. Anyone joining the Nazi Party in the expectation of engaging in discussions over policy issues would have been very quickly disappointed. The average party activist was expected to be a foot soldier, devoted to the leader, willing to carry out instructions, without comment. In order to further encourage party discipline at all levels of the party, central office created 'State Inspectors' in 1932, who had the power to investigate local party organisations. In addition, there was also an 'Investigation and Mediation Committee (USCHLA), which operated as a national tribunal to arbitrate over any disputes at the local level, and had the power to expel individuals and close down local party organisations.

The Nazi Party also created a host of ancillary organisations, including National Socialist leagues of teachers, doctors, students, civil servants, farmers, youth and women. The four most important ancillary organisations of the

Gau: District

Gauleiter: District leader of the Nazi Party. A very powerful figure within local Nazi parties. As Hitler appointed each *Gauleiter,* he was able to exert important influence over local parties. After 1933, the *Gauleiter* system was added to the local government system in Nazi Germany.

Nazi Party before 1933 were: the Stormtroopers (SA), the Hitler Youth, the National Socialist Factory Cell Organisation (NSBO) and the Agricultural Affairs Bureau. The Stormtroopers (*Sturmabteiling*), led by Ernst Röhm, consisted of ex-soldiers, who not only protected Nazi meetings, but also provided a strong army of committed – and very violent – activists to place out on the streets in direct competition against the communists. The SA had been the heart of the pre-1923 party, but it was banned by the German government in the aftermath of the failed Munich putsch. The SA was more firmly established in urban areas, and its members tended to come from the more 'socialist' and 'anti-capitalist' wing of the party. It was only in the late 1920s that the SA was allowed to operate again, but only on the condition it remained a purely non-military body. The leaders of the SA remained sceptical about the 'parliamentary' and 'legal' route to power, and remained wedded to the idea of overthrowing Weimar democracy by force. The rank and file of the SA accepted their role as the 'foot soldiers' of the movement with great reluctance, primarily because they were dependent on financial support from the party. The members of the SA had a romantic allegiance towards Hitler as leader, but they were never completely under the control of central office. The SA viewed the concentration on winning elections – especially after 1930 – as a sign that its own position within the party as a street-fighting force was being downgraded and marginalised. Between 1929 and 1933, the membership of the SA grew from 30,000 to 425,000. Most members were males between 18 and 35. The SA offered an outlet for many delinquent young men to channel their anti-social and violent proclivities against political opponents, particularly in the major cities. The SA hardly ever attacked the police during demonstrations, and they generally goaded their left-wing opponents to start a fight by parading in a highly provocative manner through areas where their political opponents lived. Hitler wanted the SA to 'conquer the streets' by out-shouting and generally making life diffi-cult for their most hated political opponents: the communists. It was often extremely difficult to restrain the hot blooded and violent elements in the SA, who doubted whether the 'parliamentary' road to power was the right road to travel along. One demand the SA sought (but which Hitler opposed) was for their members to be afforded dominance in military matters over the regular army, should the Nazis gain power. Hitler never really moulded the SA into the obedient 'political' army he wanted it to be. Indeed, the blood purge of the SA, ordered by Hitler in the summer of 1934 – under pressure from the army – was not entirely unpredictable, given the troubled relation-ship which existed between the SA and the political leadership of the party before 1933.

The Nazi Party was very successful in attracting young people, and created its own organisations for them, most notably, the Hitler Youth

Hitler-Jugend: Hitler
Youth. This organisation
became a very important
means of bringing young
people into the Nazi Party.
After 1933, the Hitler
Youth became a key Nazi
youth movement, which
every young German was
required to join.

(*Hitler-Jugend*), which indoctrinated young members of the party with Nazi
ideas on race, discipline and military values. The Nazi Party offered the young
a seemingly brighter future, which appears to have attracted many of them to
support the party. By the summer of 1932, the Hitler Youth boasted 100,000
members, with most of these recruits coming from younger members of the
middle classes. Indeed, the Hitler Youth started to incorporate the members
of traditional middle-class and lower-middle-class youth groups into its organisation as Nazi popularity increased. It sent young people to summer camps
at which physical fitness, rifle practice, and team-building games were high
on the agenda. The German Girls' League, a female equivalent organisation,
encouraged young girls to improve their fitness, but mostly concentrated on
developing the domestic skills required of a future wife and mother. The
Hitler Youth mobilised large numbers of young people, and created a close
camaraderie among its members. Members of the Hitler Youth before 1933 later
recalled that 'no social or class distinctions' operated within the organisation
(Allen, 1995: 73).

The Agricultural Affairs Bureau, another important Nazi ancillary organisation, led by Richard Darre, helped to persuade farmers and agricultural
workers to support the Nazi Party. It provided expert commentary, specialist
speakers on agricultural matters, and established a newspaper (*National-
Sozialistische Landpost*), with a wide circulation in farming regions. The Nazi
Party promised to introduce significant land reform to help drag farmers
out of the 'great depression'. The specialised work of the Agricultural Affairs
Bureau constantly highlighted the sorry plight of farmers. It appears this
strategy did pay dividends, as the growth in Nazi electoral support from 1930
onwards was higher in rural areas, especially in places where the Agricultural
Affairs Bureau had been most active.

The Nazi Party also attempted, with much less success, to gain support from
members of the industrial working class by creating the National Socialist
Factory Cell Organisation (NSBO) during the early 1930s. The idea of setting
up grass-roots supporters of Nazism among factory workers emanated
from the more 'socialist' wing of the party, predominantly based in northern
regions of Germany. In the spring of 1931, Gregor Strasser launched the 'Into
the Factories' campaign, which aimed to increase working-class support for
the Nazi Party in industrial areas. Towards the end of 1932, 250,000 workers
were members of the NSBO. Yet Hitler refused to support the establishment
of Nazi trade union organisations, which tended to weaken greatly the appeal
of the NSBO among factory workers. Indeed, when the Nazis came to power,
most trade union rights were removed, and the NSBO, because it ignored the
wishes of the employer – and favoured those of the employee – was deemed
as incompatible with National Socialist ideology, and forced to disband. It
was replaced under Nazi rule by the Labour Front (DAF), led by Robert Ley,

which aimed to create 'a social and productive community' which defined the employer as 'master' and the employee as 'follower'.

There is little doubt that the Nazi Party, although not free of factional rivalries and disagreements, did possess a very efficient centralised organisational apparatus. It also possessed a leader whose speaking powers were a match for any other party. There were also many figures within the party, most notably, Goebbels and Strasser, who had great propaganda and organisational skills, which were also the envy of other parties. In addition, the party had many committed and self-sacrificing local leaders and activists, a strong group of paramilitary supporters in the SA willing to engage in violence with political opponents, and a growing youth movement.

PROPAGANDA

A second key factor, which greatly contributed to the rise to power of the Nazi Party was effective propaganda. In *Mein Kampf*, Hitler devoted two chapters to propaganda. According to Hitler, the mass of the people, about whom he had a very low opinion, could be easily influenced by means of the constant repetition of a number of key slogans and images of effective propaganda. Nazi propaganda was centrally controlled and organised by Dr Joseph Goebbels (the original 'spin doctor'), who was appointed head of Party Propaganda in November 1928. It was, in fact, no coincidence that the great surge in Nazi electoral support took place in the period after Goebbels took control of Nazi Party propaganda.

At the heart of Nazi propaganda was the spoken word, delivered in its most powerful form by Adolf Hitler, whose speeches, using microphones and loudspeakers, became a major focal point of the appeal of the Nazi Party to electors. At party rallies and public meetings, Hitler's entrance was always delayed – to build up the tension slowly. When he appeared, he was accompanied by a torchlight procession by flag-bearing and drum-beating supporters, while music played and searchlights flashed all around the arena. Hitler presented himself in his speeches as a humble soldier whose life work was to restore the honour of Germany. The Nuremberg rally, held annually from 1927 onwards, was a quasi-religious event: organised with great theatrical flair, which helped to give a powerful display of Nazi passion [Doc. 15, p. 122].

Yet stage-managed Nazi rallies, at which Hitler appeared, were only one important aspect of Nazi propaganda activity. The Nazi message was relayed by a large number of party-appointed public speakers at meetings held throughout the country. Some of the other leading Nazis – particularly Goebbels – gained a high reputation as orators, but it was a large band of specialist speakers who carried the Nazi message into local areas. All speakers were required to undertake training, and required authorisation from central office before they were allowed to operate. Registered Nazi-approved speakers were required – even when qualified – to submit the text of their speeches to national party headquarters for final approval. The Nazis often employed former army officers, U-boat captains, farmers, teachers and even some pastors to give speeches. Joseph Goebbels kept local branches supplied with up-to-date information on key electoral issues and often gave instructions as to how local party workers were to present issues to potential voters [**Doc. 19, p. 125**]. One of the greatest strengths of Nazi propaganda was the way local speakers were allowed to tailor their message to reflect policies and fears and prejudices of importance in different areas of the country. Another innovative aspect of Nazi propaganda activity at the local level was the holding of meetings not only before and during elections, but also in the time between them. This active form of campaigning meant the Nazi Party – unlike its leading political opponents – was always permanently attempting to reinforce solidarity among existing supporters and to attract new converts.

The Nazi Party also created a key visual propaganda symbol: the Nazi flag, which proved extremely effective. The Nazi flag with its distinctive and visually memorable Swastika logo – designed by Hitler – was a potent symbol of party identity. It was basically red, borrowing that colour from the popular communist red flag, but in its centre was a white circle – to represent the pure Aryan heritage – with the visually memorable black Swastika symbol, borrowed from earlier *Volkisch* sects, in the centre. The flag ingeniously incorporated the red of socialism with the traditional black and white of the pre-1914 imperial flag.

Goebbels also created many memorable posters, which included such key Nazi slogans as: 'Hitler – Germany's last chance', 'One People, One Nation, One Leader' (*ein Volk, ein Reich, ein Führer*), and 'Germany Awake'. Nazi posters always depicted workers in favourable terms, but portrayed communists usually as bearded 'foreigners', with definite Semitic looks, manipulating the workers for their own ends. Most democratic politicians, especially those associated with the 'betrayal' of Germany during the war were shown in Nazi posters as fat hypocrites, dining on champagne and caviar. Most Nazi electoral posters were anti-Marxist and anti-communist, while most anti-Semitic posters were confined to Nazi newspapers. In many rural areas, Nazi propaganda had a free run as neither the Communist Party, which had few supporters in such areas, nor the traditional democratic parties, bothered to use propaganda heavily in these areas.

The Nazi Party also used the press – with much less success – to spread its gospel to potential followers. Hitler believed the press was of great importance in helping to mould public opinion. To this end, the Nazis set up a number of 'in house' newspapers, including, a national daily newspaper (the *Völkischer Beobachter*), and many other local newspapers, most notably, *The Attack* (*Der Angriff*) based in Berlin. However, the sales of Nazi newspapers were poor. In September 1930, for example, sales of the *Völkischer Beobachter* were 100,000. Nazi newspapers were quite good at creating blood-curdling headlines, and often used photographs effectively, but in general the quality of the journalism was poor. Nazi newspapers concentrated on a very small number of themes, and the articles in them were written in a very uninspiring and repetitive manner. After 1930, the Nazis benefitted from receiving very favourable coverage in many of the leading regional papers controlled by Alfred Hugenberg, the leader of the conservative National People's Party (DNVP).

The Nazis – in power – are always associated with the effective use of film in propaganda, in which they are often seen – especially in modern TV documentaries – to be ahead of their time. Before 1933, however, the Nazi Party, even though it established the National Socialist Film Service in 1928, did not make extensive use of film in its propaganda activities. The Nazis did show some propaganda films, using party-owned projectors and screens, in some remote rural areas during election campaigns. We also know that the newsreel company *Ufa*, owned by Hugenberg, allowed the Nazis a platform in many of the newsreels shown in cinemas throughout Germany during the early 1930s. However, the actual number of times Adolf Hitler appeared in newsreels was limited, and film cannot be viewed as a major aspect of Nazi propaganda before 1933. In fact, many of the existing German democratic parties, most notably, the liberal German Democratic Party (DDP) and the German National People's Party (DNVP) made much greater use of film than did the Nazi Party.

It is important to examine some of the key themes of Nazi Party propaganda. In attacking their opponents, the Nazis were great exponents of what is now called 'negative campaigning'. The Nazis blamed the economic depression and high unemployment on the failings of the Weimar democratic system. The 'Marxists' (and to a lesser extent 'Jews') were depicted in Nazi propaganda as the key enemies of the German people. Alongside this 'negative campaigning', the Nazis emphasised the positive aspects of their own 'Movement'. Above all, Nazi propaganda projected Hitler as the charismatic saviour of the German people. Indeed, such was the dominance of Hitler in the projection of the Nazi Party, it became commonplace for most German newspapers, and most political opponents, to describe the party in articles and speeches as 'the Hitler movement'.

A great many historians would suggest Nazi propaganda appealed most persuasively to the middle classes. There was a distinct change in the focus of Nazi propaganda after 1928, away from attempting to appeal to the 'workers' in urban centres, and towards targeting middle-class voters, especially those in rural areas, with no strong pre-existing political allegiances [**Doc. 14, p. 121**]. The Nazis also tried to win over the working classes, and kept on stressing the broad 'national' appeal of their programme, but it became increasingly apparent to Nazi activists that their appeals to patriotism, a strong leader, anti-Marxism, and the creation of a folk community were being received far more sympathetically in middle-class areas of the cities, and in rural areas.

MEMBERSHIP

The social profile of members of the Nazi Party has been the subject of detailed scrutiny among historians. The most dominant view, in this debate, suggests the Nazi Party was dominated by the middle classes, or more specifically, the lower middle class. In more recent times, however, this view has been challenged by a counter-argument which suggests the Nazi Party was a genuine 'people's party' whose membership was drawn from all social groups in German society, with a substantial working-class element.

The Nazi Party began life – as we have already seen – as an anti-parliamentary and revolutionary antidote to the growing appeal of socialism among the working classes. It was envisaged – at the outset – as an alternative to existing socialist parties, which appealed to the working classes, such as the Social Democratic Party (SPD) and the Communist Party (KPD). Yet the Nazi Party never attracted a sizeable number of converts as members from either of these parties. Very few active communists, socialists, trade unionists, or factory workers, located in the major urban centres, ever joined the Nazi Party. On the contrary, these people proved the most hostile towards the party and relatively immune from its appeal.

The membership of the early Nazi Party, located in Munich from 1919 to 1923, was dominated by males from middle-class and lower-middle-class groups, most notably, skilled independent craftsmen, small businessmen, merchants, office workers, low-ranking civil servants, teachers and farmers. Very few women ever became official party members, nor were they encouraged to join. By and large, the early members of the Nazi Party consisted of people – even those within the middle class – who were anti-parliamentary, and most often politically adrift from the mainstream democratic political parties. It is also noticeable in the early membership lists of the Nazi Party how many 'renegade' members of the upper middle class, the former aristocracy, and university students keep appearing. Most of these members viewed the Nazi Party as a potential counter-revolutionary movement, which could restore their pre-1914 position within German society by destroying democracy. These upper-middle-class supporters were more likely to be old style conservatives, and the natural supporters of right-wing nationalist and conservative parties. Much less prominent on the membership lists of the party in its early days were industrial 'unskilled workers'. Indeed, this group, even though the party called itself a 'Workers' Party' formed a minority among its membership even during its early years in Munich. The Nazi Party was much more successful in attracting the disgruntled skilled worker, or self-employed independent artisan, because these workers viewed themselves as a cut above the level of the 'proletarian' worker, and the prejudices against Jews, which the Nazis emphasised, were already prominent in these groups, but much less pronounced among the working classes. As one historian puts it: 'fascism was the socialism of the petit-bourgeosie' (Fischer, 1995: 91).

In the period from 1924 to 1929 – when the Nazi Party became a more nationally based party – there was a sharp increase in membership. The greatest proportion of new members in this period came from the Protestant middle class, the petit bourgeois lower middle class and small landholding groups. More small businessmen and small independent skilled workers joined the party between 1924 to 1928. Among this group it was the owners of small and medium-sized firms and wholesalers rather than those who owned large factories who became members.

After 1928, largely due to the efforts of successful propaganda, the Nazi Party started to attract increasing numbers of members among small farmers. It seems many of these farmers had not owed allegiance to any other political party before they joined the Nazis and were attracted by the Nazi idea of a folk community, in which agricultural self-sufficiency would be a central aim. Farmers – and agricultural workers – started to view the Nazi Party as a potential saviour of the agricultural sector. It was also in the period from 1928 onwards that the Nazi Party started to attract growing numbers of the new middle class of white-collar workers, lower-grade civil servants, and middle-class professionals. The Nazi Party also continued to attract teachers, even though they were subject to possible disciplinary action – even dismissal – for joining the party. The Nazi Party membership lists after 1928 contain larger numbers of the upper middle classes. In 1930, 50 per cent of all German university students were members of the party, which seems a surprisingly high figure, as the Nazi Party was a very anti-intellectual party, which showed contempt for 'book learned academics'.

The Nazi Party continued to make energetic efforts to attract new working-class members in heavily industrialised areas, but such workers remained relatively immune to these initiatives. By and large, the industrial working class were not attracted, except in very small and isolated pockets, to join the Nazi Party. Those 'workers' who did join the party tended to come from small towns and villages, without a strong tradition of socialism. The Nazi 'working-class' member tended to resemble 'working-class conservatives' in Britain, and identified with the middle classes. Overall, the Nazi Party, although it did attract more 'workers' in the period from 1924 to 1930, continued to be a predominantly lower-middle-class party, which was becoming increasingly more attractive to the upper class, small businessmen, white collar workers and people who lived in small towns and villages, without any strong political allegiance to any of the traditional parties.

It was in the period from 1930 to 1933 when Nazi Party membership – and electoral support – increased sharply. It was during this period when the party, though it still insisted it spoke for 'all national groups', began to cater its propaganda towards the traditional concerns of middle-class Germans, and attempted to attract rural members in larger numbers. In this period, the backbone of the Nazi Party continued to be members from the lower middle class, although the percentage of new members from this group tended to be lower than it had been from 1924 to 1930. The group which greatly increased its membership of the party came from the upper middle class, and the former aristocracy. Many of these new members came from 'old' conservative middle-class groups – already hostile towards the Weimar republic – who started to view the Nazi Party as a viable alternative to the traditional right-wing German People's Party (DNVP). It is also noticeable – after 1929 – how Hitler began to downgrade the 'socialist' aspects of the Nazi programme, in favour of the 'nationalistic' elements. There was a definite increase in support from small businessmen and even some major industrialists such as Fritz Thyseen, Hugo Stinnes and Albert Vögler after 1930, though this group remained under-represented in the party as a whole. Many large landowning farmers started to join the party. They appear to have been attracted by the Nazi promise to give the revival of agriculture a top priority within the new national community. The Nazi Party was also successful in attracting growing numbers of upper-middle-class professionals, and high ranking civil servants to join the party from 1930 onwards. There is little doubt that something very significant was happening among some sections of the Protestant German middle classes during the period after 1930: many were increasingly attracted to the Nazi Party, believing that its promise to give aid to farmers and protection for business from foreign competition could drag Germany out of political and economic crisis [**Doc. 17, p. 124**]. Yet the appeal of the Nazis did not attract all members of the middle class. The Catholic parts of Germany, which accounted for a third of the population, were not receptive to the Nazi Party and remained loyal to the Catholic Centre Party. Hence, if Nazism was a middle-class revolt, it was a Protestant one.

The Nazi Party also attracted its largest influx of 'workers' between 1930 and 1933. For the first time, the Nazi Party did gain more converts from former supporters of the SPD in industrial areas, than it had ever done before. At the same time, the polarisation between Nazis and communists became much stronger than ever before, with their street battles in big cities becoming a serious law and order problem.

From 1930 to 1933, the Nazi Party attracted a broader spectrum of support than at any time in its history. It is also true that in 1932 approximately 40 per cent of party members came from working-class backgrounds. There were certainly more working-class members joining the party after 1930 than in any other period. However, when attention is focused more closely on these new 'working-class' members of the party, it can be seen that most were craft workers, agricultural labourers and those workers employed in small companies, without a strong trade union presence. The Nazi Party still encountered difficulties, even at the height of its pre-1933 electoral popularity, in attracting factory workers, who were also members of trade unions, in the major urban industrial centres. It was workers who felt above the level of a 'proletarian', and those who were antagonistic towards socialism who joined the party. These 'working-class Nazis' possessed upwardly mobile aspirations. It seems most of these 'workers' shifted their support from the non-socialist parties, and right-wing 'nationalist' fringe groups rather than from either the communists or the Social Democrats, although the Nazis did gain some converts from these groups. It is often thought the Nazi Party prospered on the discontent of the unemployed. Yet the Communist Party attracted more support from the urban unemployed during the early 1930s, than the Nazis. Indeed, the Nazis gained more support from white-collar workers, civil servants and professionals who were still in work, but feared they might become unemployed. In rural areas, the Nazis were able to mobilise 'workers' who seemingly had no previous political allegiance to any political party. Most urban industrialised and unionised workers did not join the Nazi Party. In rural Protestant communities, especially in the north, large numbers of agricultural labourers joined the party. Again, this group had very little affinity with socialism, or any strong pre-existing allegiance to trade unions. New recruits in rural areas seem to have been attracted by the idea, put forward in Nazi propaganda, that a Nazi government would bring about a 'new deal' for rural Germany [Doc. 14, p. 121]. Most new recruits to the Nazi party (48.6 per cent) from 1930 onwards came from the middle class. At the same time, the upper middle class were joining the party in far higher numbers than ever before. Many of the existing working-class members – especially those in the SA – were very alarmed about the increasingly 'bourgeois' direction in which the party was moving in 1930.

It must be accepted that the lower middle class and middle class were always over-represented among the membership of the Nazi Party. Indeed, judged on the basis of party membership, it can be argued that it was predominantly a lower-middle-class party, which extended its solid core from 1930 onwards to incorporate greater numbers of the upper middle classes, and attracted many new working-class supporters and 'workers' in rural areas. At the same time, it must be emphasised that the Nazi Party attracted a broader cross-section of members than any other Weimar political party. This can be ascribed in a very great measure to Hitler's clever political ploy of attempting to portray the party as a more respectable 'nationalist' and 'conservative' party, willing to work within the existing system, and to down-play its previous ambiguous relationship with 'socialism' and its former allegiance towards the violent overthrow of the state.

6

The Nazi Breakthrough, 1925–1930

A NEW DIRECTION

At the end of 1924, the future of the Nazi Party seemed almost hopeless. Adolf Hitler, its most famous figure, had only just been released from prison on strict parole for 'high treason'. He was prohibited from speaking in most parts of Germany until 1927 and this ban was not lifted in Prussia until 1928. Hitler feared being deported back to the country of his birth. On 7 April 1925, he renounced his Austrian citizenship, but did not officially become a German citizen until 1932. Hitler had placed Alfred Rosenberg in charge of the party in his absence, but he proved incapable of establishing any authority and the party split into two rival factions during his absence: (i) The Greater German People's Party, which included the nucleus of the Munich branch of the party and (ii) the National Socialist Freedom Party, composed of the more 'socialist' elements in northern Germany. The only consolation for Hitler was that both factions continued to pledge allegiance towards his leadership. During his confinement Hitler had time to rethink his political strategy. He became convinced that trying to bring about an armed 'seizure of power' had clearly failed and so he decided to abandon it. The only way the Nazi Party would now come to power was by legal means gained through electoral success [**Doc. 7, p. 115**]. Hitler explained his new strategy to Karl Ludecke, a close aide, while in prison: 'When I resume active work it will be necessary to pursue a new policy. Instead of working to achieve power by armed coup, we shall have to hold our noses and enter the Reichstag (Shirer, 1961: 151). Such a strategy was likely to prove a long-drawn out process with no certainty of success. The only optimistic news to lift Hitler's gloom at this time was the decision on 16 February 1925 of Frantz Gürtner, the Bavarian Justice Minister, to lift the ban on the Nazi Party and on 26 February the party newspaper, *Völkischer Beobachter*, reappeared with a long editorial written by Hitler entitled: 'A New Beginning' in which he promised to 'work within the constitution'.

REBUILDING THE NAZI PARTY

At a party meeting on 27 February 1925, Hitler made public his decision to pursue a 'legal path to power' and promised to work within the constitution. Hitler knew it was no easy task to transform the Nazi Party from a rabble-rousing, street-fighting force into a national party, with an efficient national organisation quickly. He insisted the SA be reorganised and subordinated to the party leader. He worked steadily to undermine the prestige of his biggest rival on the far right, General Ludendorff, who had founded the nationalistic Tannenberg League. Ludendorff's credibility was deeply damaged by his decision to stand for the Presidency in 1925 against Hindenburg, in which he received a derisory one per cent of the vote. From this point on Ludendorff was condemned to complete irrelevance and faded from the scene.

Hitler's decision to take the parliamentary road to power was a pragmatic and tactical one. The Nazi Party did not become democratic in aims, ideology or organisation at all. Hitler told his supporters he wanted to remain the unconditional and all-powerful leader of the party. Munich would also remain the centre of all party activities. The loyal rank and file in the Bavarian capital welcomed Hitler back as undisputed 'Führer' with few voices of dissent. Outside Bavaria, Hitler had more trouble reasserting his previous dictatorial authority. He knew that if the Nazi Party was to become truly national it needed a strong footing in the north. So he sent Gregor Strasser, a skilful young organiser from Bavaria to try and improve recruitment in urban, working-class areas by drawing attention to the 'socialist' aspects of the party programme. Membership in the north soon increased fourfold largely due to Gregor Strasser's energetic efforts. These new members owed little allegiance to Hitler. Many had not met him or seen him speak. A debate now ensued in the party on what was the best electoral strategy for the reinvented party. The northern wing had always been more 'socialist' and 'anti-capitalist' in outlook. These young radicals believed Hitler was a 'soldier radical', more in tune with their 'progressive' and 'socialist' ideas than the views of the largely counter-revolutionary reactionaries surrounding him in Munich, many of whom were closely aligned with renegade members of the upper classes and the army. One of the strongest 'socialist' radicals was Dr Joseph Goebbels, who had already proved an effective speaker, propagandist and party organiser in the industrial Rhineland. Goebbels wanted the Nazi Party to become more 'socialist' and felt the best potential vote-winning electoral strategy was to compete for votes in the large urban and industrial areas against the socialist working class and trade union orientated parties: the SPD and the KPD [Doc. 8, p. 116].

The northern group next came out in favour of a policy designed to confiscate the land of the deposed Hohenzollern princes and redistribute it to local peasants. This proved too radical for Hitler and he strongly opposed it. Hitler felt the 'socialist' strategy as a whole would alienate potential middle-class voters and antagonise the conservative groups with whom it would be necessary to collaborate in order to gain power.

To resolve this dispute, Hitler called a meeting composed of members of the northern and southern wings of the party at Bamberg – a city very close to Munich – on 14 February 1926. He packed it with his loyal cronies. Only Goebbels and Strasser were able to attend from the northern branches. The real issue at stake at Bamberg was whether the Nazi Party would remain a 'Führer' party, in which the leader's authority was undisputed or whether power would derive from the party programme, which could be democratically altered by pressure from factions within the various regional sections of the party. Hitler gained full acceptance for the principle that he was the undisputed leader. He gained another important pledge to retain the existing 1920 party programme as 'unalterable', by arguing it contained firm commitments to several 'socialist' policies already. As the 'expropriation' of monarchical land was not included in that programme, Hitler asked the northern wing to drop support for this policy, as a means of expressing public unity within the party – and they duly agreed. By the spring of 1926, Hitler had re-established firm control over the Nazi Party. It was a pretty hollow victory really. All he had accomplished was the right to lead what remained a very small and insignificant political party, which seemed to have precious little prospect of becoming a major force in German politics. A far more significant outcome of the Bamberg meeting was that Hitler had gained the firm support of Goebbels, who now became a loyal ally and soon emerged as a quite brilliant electoral strategist and propagandist.

For a party whose very life-blood was misery and despair the economic conditions in Germany between 1924 and 1929 were worryingly optimistic. It seemed springtime for Weimar and Germany had finally arrived after a long winter of discontent. Unemployment fell below a million, the currency stabilised, wages increased, retail sales were up by 20 per cent, wages went up by 10 per cent and the dreaded inflation was finally brought under control. To the outside world, Germany appeared re-born and transformed, with a thriving economy and a vibrant and free spirited 'Cabaret' nightlife in the big cities. In 1926, Germany joined the League of Nations, accepted the western territorial arrangements of the Paris peace settlement under the Locarno Treaties and was even making regular reparations payments. The money that fuelled this prosperity came from seven billion US dollars' worth of loans. No one gave much thought about whether Germany could afford the repayments either in the short or long term.

THE STRANGE MYSTERY OF HITLER AND GELI RAUBAL

Hitler's 'Years in the Wilderness' between 1925 and 1929 were in many ways the happiest of his life. He lived in several inns in the picturesque market village of Berchtesgaden before renting a nearby villa ['The Berghof'] high up the Obersalzberg Mountains. 'I spent there the finest hours of my life', he claimed in 1942 (Shirer, 1961: 164). Nearing forty, there was still no sign of romance in his life. In 1929, Hitler rented a luxurious nine-room apartment in Munich on Prinzregentenstrasse, but continued to spend far more time at the 'Berghof'. Hitler took on his widowed half-sister Angela Raubal as his housekeeper in both residences. She brought along her two daughters – Geli and Friedl. Geli Raubal was twenty in 1928, when she came to live with 'Uncle Dolf' as she called Hitler. Geli was very attractive, with strong features, long blonde hair, and a bubbly, vibrant personality. Hitler took Geli to many social events and was seemingly besotted with her. Maybe Hitler wanted a romantic involvement with Geli? There is no real evidence that any sexual relations took place between the two. The following facts are known. Geli was observed showing jealousy when Hitler showed interest in other women at parties they attended together. It's clear Hitler was far more overly protective of Geli than is healthy for an uncle. He became agitated when she became close to Emil Maurice, his bodyguard and chauffeur, and he promptly sacked him. On 17 September 1931, neighbours overheard a blazing row between Hitler and Geli at his Munich apartment. It concerned Hitler's opposition to his niece wanting to return to Vienna for a course of singing lessons. Geli reportedly leaned out of a first floor window and shouted down at Hitler, as he walked towards his limousine: 'So you won't let me go to Vienna?', to which he angrily replied, 'No!' The next day, Geli Raubal was found dead in her room in the apartment. The coroner concluded she took her own life by shooting herself with a single shot, aimed at her heart. There were rumours, mainly in the left-wing press, that Hitler had killed Geli in a jealous rage. This can be ruled out. Hitler was in Hamburg that evening. Of all the possible scenarios, and there have been many, suicide is the most likely cause of her death. Hitler was struck down by uncontrollable grief in the days which followed. His close aides later recounted that Geli was, apart from his mother, the only other human being the Nazi leader ever truly loved. Eva Braun was more or less told by the Nazi dictator that 'no one can match my Geli'. Hitler's strange obsession continued long after she died. He kept her room in his Munich flat, and the one at the Berghof, exactly as she had left them before she died. The extraordinary passion and the strange morbid grieving Hitler exhibited towards Geli Raubal remains one of the central personal mysteries of Hitler's life in the period before he came to power and one that has never been fully explained. Did Geli's death play some part in altering Hitler's personality and making him more inhumane? It's a very interesting question, but one which is impossible to answer given the lack of evidence on Hitler's psychological feelings.

THE EMERGENCE OF A NEW NAZI PARTY ELECTION STRATEGY

In the period after 1926 there was a pressing need for the Nazi Party to decide how it was going to appeal to voters in democratic elections. Focusing exclusively on Hitler's charismatic speaking abilities was not an option, as the speaking ban on the Nazi leader remained in force until September 1928. The 'socialist' north German elements persuaded a somewhat sceptical Hitler to adopt what became known as 'The Urban Plan', in 1926. This concentrated on trying to increase electoral support in major industrial cities. To this end, the Nazi Party adopted a strident 'anti-capitalist' tone in its electioneering which persistently attacked finance capitalists and the 'decadence' of the upper-middle-class parties that supported the Weimar Republic. The achieve-ments of the Urban Plan were extremely few and far between. The great majority of industrial workers in the major urban areas continued to vote in elections for the KPD and SPD. The image of the Nazis in such areas remained that of a right-wing party determined to crush 'progressive', truly anti-capitalist revolutionary socialism. The arrival of the Nazis in working-class areas was usually the starting point of a violent street battle. At the beginning of 1928, Hitler, who was deeply sceptical about the likely success of winning over the working classes to National Socialism anyway, first downgraded, and then abandoned the Urban Plan. The Nazi Party did not completely give up trying to win working-class voters but what emerged – largely under Hitler's prompting – was a new and more sophisticated and targeted electoral strategy which involved attracting greater middle-class support, placing much greater emphasis on winning over disaffected and first time voters in Protestant rural areas in north Germany, while still maintaining a presence in working-class industrial areas, but lowering the importance of that priority from what had been envisaged in the days of the Urban Plan. In the first National Election the Nazi Party faced on 20 May 1928, using its new democratic electoral strategy, the results were extremely disappointing, in spite of all the marching, fighting and demonstrating that Nazi activists had displayed during the campaign. The Nazis gained 810,000 votes – 0.8 per cent of the electors, which gave them a measly 12 seats in the Reichstag. This was actually a fall of 100,000 voters from the previous election. The results in industrial areas were dire, but in some rural areas in the north the Nazi Party polled 18 per cent, thus showing that in farming areas their message was striking a chord with voters. After the 1928 election the party revamped its propaganda appeal to the farming community, promising voters in rural areas a 'special position' in the Third Reich. In June 1929, the Nazi Party made impressive gains in local elections and won control of their first local council in Coburg. There were already clear signs that a major Nazi breakthrough might be possible in the rural areas the traditional parties ignored. There was also one additional asset the party had regained. Hitler was now able to give public speeches across the country. The Nazi party had regained its biggest electioneering asset – Hitler's voice. None of this could hide the fact that the Nazi Party remained a fringe party. It would need something remarkable to change this.

THE IMPACT OF 'THE GREAT DEPRESSION'

On 24 October 1929, known as 'Black Thursday', there was a sudden outburst of panic selling of shares on the New York Stock exchange on Wall Street. Five days later, on 29 October, 'Black Tuesday', the crisis deepened. Over 16.4 billon shares were sold in one frenetic day. Between 1929 and 1932, the New York share index fell from 452 to 58 points. American banks withdrew funds rapidly from Germany and the economy completely collapsed. Production fell by nearly 50 per cent. Thousands of small businesses and farms went out of business. By 1931, German banks came perilously close to collapse and a major Austrian bank fell. The number of registered unemployed rose from 1.6 million in 1929 to 6.12 million by February 1932. Around 33 per cent of the entire workforce lost their jobs during this period. When the effect of unemployment on whole families is taken into account, around 23 million Germans were affected by the 'Great Depression'. The economic downturn hit bankers, businessmen, industrial workers, farmers, small shopkeepers, workers in light industry, pensioners, white-collar workers and members of the middle-class professions. The misery of the German people, most with fresh memories of the 'great inflation', was profound and clearly affected the political atmosphere between 1930 and 1933.

Hindenburg refused to allow Herman Müller, the SPD Chancellor, the opportunity to rule by 'Emergency Decree'. On 27 March 1930, the last Weimar coalition based on a mixture of the democratic parties fell from power. The coalition had collapsed after failing to agree whether unemployment benefits could be maintained or should be cut. Though few Germans realised it at the time, this really was the beginning of the end of democratic government in Germany. From 1930 onwards, no government ruled with the support of a parliamentary majority in the Reichstag. Each German Chancellor was personally appointed and stayed in power with the consent of President Hindenburg, under the arbitrary emergency powers allotted to him under Article 48 of the constitution. Heinrich Brüning, a member of the Catholic Centre Party became the new Chancellor in March 1930. He was an austere character, who had built his reputation by specialising on financial matters. As a former army officer, he wanted a restoration of the German monarchy and a reduction of the power of the Reichstag. Two leading army figures – General Wilhelm Groener, the Minister of Defence and his close political adviser General Kurt von Schleicher, a friend of Hindenburg's son Oskar – had both recommended Brüning as Chancellor. Schleicher, a vain and unscrupulous political intriguer, played – we shall see shortly – a key role in the coming to power of Hitler. He felt that in a period of severe government cuts the new Chancellor would protect spending on the army – and he was proved right.

THE EMERGENCE OF HITLER ON THE NATIONAL STAGE

Adolf Hitler now skilfully exploited the many political opportunities the gloomy economic circumstances opened up for the Nazi Party. Hitler's decision – taken before the economic collapse – to concentrate on winning over middle-class support, especially in rural areas, proved a masterstroke. The Nazi leader who had long predicted economic catastrophe now offered Germans hope of deliverance from misery. Hitler's faith in the German people and his supreme optimism that a regeneration of Germany could only occur under his leadership struck a remarkable chord. At the heart of that appeal was his contention that the Nazi Party was the only true 'national' party **[Doc. 17, p. 124]**.

Hitler's national profile was already growing before the Wall Street crash. In March 1929, at the trial of three young army officers accused of spreading Nazi propaganda in the army, Hitler distanced himself from their activities and once more emphasised that the Nazi Party would come to power democratically. During the summer of 1929 Hitler collaborated with several other right-wing groups, most notably, the Pan-Germans, the Agrarian League and the DNVP led by Alfred Hugenberg, during a national referendum campaign against the US-sponsored Young Plan – a reduced scale of reparations payments – designed to replace the 1924 Dawes Plan. With the help of Hugenberg's powerful newsreel company (*Ufa*), his newspaper interests and business allies, Hitler gained important publicity for his first major national speaking tour. Even though the campaign ended in failure, Hitler had received extensive national publicity. Even respectable conservative newspapers were predicting that Hitler was a potential unifier of the previously leaderless and discredited German right.

There remained some members of the Nazi Party who continued to press for a more definite 'socialist' commitment by Hitler. These divisions erupted into a public debate in 1930 between Hitler and Otto Strasser, one of the leading figures in the 'anti-capitalist' grouping within the party and brother of Gregor. Otto Strasser believed the Nazi Party was being transformed by Hitler, turning into a respectable, pro-capitalist, anti-Marxist, middle-class party which increasingly viewed the working class as the enemy. Hitler claimed his 'National socialism' was markedly different from the communist anti-capitalist version. 'I have never said that all enterprises should be socialised', Hitler said. 'On the contrary, I have maintained that we might socialise enterprises prejudicial to the interests of the state'. Otto Strasser concluded that Hitler's pro-capitalist version of socialism differed little from the reactionary version of the traditional conservative right [**Doc. 11, p. 118**]. The Hitler–Strasser debate helped ease the worries of potential business and middle-class voters, as Hitler indicated that 'National Socialism' posed no real threat to the capitalist owners of industry and promised no state ownership or high taxes on the rich. On the contrary, Hitler had raised the prospect that the Nazi Party could forge an alliance with the forces of the traditional right.

THE NAZI ELECTORAL BREAKTHROUGH IN 1930

In July 1930, the Reichstag rejected Brüning's first attempt to rule by Presidential decree. New elections were set for 14 September. The campaign was fought in an atmosphere of extreme passion not witnessed since the early days of the Weimar Republic. Hitler went on a nationwide speaking tour. He ranted against the failure of democracy, its multiplicity of self-interested and quarrelling parties and its monumental economic failure. In place of this, he promised to make Germans strong again, end reparations payments, repudiate the Versailles Treaty, drive out 'Jewish' financiers, purge 'revolutionary parasites' on the left, help farmers, put people back to work and create a new classless 'National Community' promoting equality of opportunity. This powerful and emotional appeal was supplemented by a quite brilliant propaganda campaign, engineered by Goebbels, which targeted specific voting groups in the electorate. The Nazis produced eye-catching posters, film shows, mass rallies and torchlight parades through the streets. Door-to-door canvassers pushed the Nazi message with a passion that exceeded even the communists.

In the days before opinion polls, no one could predict the outcome. The results delivered one of the most amazing breakthroughs ever seen in a democratic election. The Nazi Party showed a remarkable surge of voter support. Their votes increased from 810,000 in 1928 to 6.4 million, representing 18 per cent of the total vote and no fewer than 107 seats in the Reichstag. In one single election the Nazi Party had advanced from insignificance to become the second most popular political party in Germany. Hitler's amazing plan to come to power legally no longer seemed like the ranting of a rabble-rousing extremist. Of the existing middle-class parties only the Centre Party increased its vote from 3.7 million to 4.1 million votes, increasing its seats in the Reichstag from 62 to 68. However, the centre and right-wing parties on which Brüning had hoped to create a right-wing leaning coalition suffered major losses. The conservative DNVP saw its share of the votes fall from 14.3 per cent to 7 per cent and saw its seats drop from 73 to 41 and the Liberal 'People's Party' went down to 31 seats from a previous total of 45. Overall, the parties who had supported Brüning before the election lost 53 of their previous combined total of 236. The parties of the left fared better. The SPD declined from 153 to 143, but remained the largest party. The Communist KPD saw its seats in the Reichstag grow from 54 to 72 and its popular vote from 10.6 per cent to 13 per cent. The biggest gainers in the election had been the two extreme parties who were both committed to doing away with democracy, and the minority Brüning government had lost a great deal of credibility. The Nazi Party was in September 1930 the second most popular party in Germany.

WHY DID THE NAZI PARTY APPEAL TO VOTERS?

Given the horrors that followed, it now seems impossible to believe that people could vote in such large numbers in democratic elections for Nazism of their own free will. Contemporaries tended to view economic misery as the key reason for the sudden surge in voting support. Herman Gerlach wrote in 1930, 'Nazi support is a mile wide, but an inch deep. If the sun shines once more on the German economy, Hitler's voters will melt away like snow' (Burleigh, 2000: 133). The Nazis undoubtedly profited from the overheated political atmosphere created by the economic depression, but the unemployed voted for the SPD and the KPD. To simply see the increase in Nazi support as a one-off 'bitterness' or 'protest' vote seems simplistic.

A great deal of credit must be given to Adolf Hitler, and the efficient Nazi Party propaganda machine in persuading voters to see the Nazis as the major outlet for their frustration with their economic circumstances and the inability of the Weimar system to cope with them. Nazi Party rallies during the election campaign were better stage-managed than those of any other party. Many 'floating voters' later recalled they felt they were being caught up in something resembling the emergence of a great passionate religious movement rather than attending a traditional democratic party rally [**Doc. 15, p. 122**].

Electoral statistics show the Nazi Party was not a 'middle-class party', but gained votes from all social groupings, age groups and regions. There were, however, some areas where Nazi support was particularly strong. Nazi voting strength was higher in the Protestant rural areas of the north German plain, stretching from east Prussia to Schleswig-Holstein, than anywhere else. In some of these regions the Nazis gained over 50 per cent of the votes. The Nazis did not just do better in small rural villages – as was previously supposed – but in larger rural areas too. Yet religious allegiance was important in deciding whether or not a German voted Nazi. Some Catholics did vote Nazi – but its appeal was less strong among them. This is evident when the election results in Catholic Bavaria are examined. Here Catholic voters stayed loyal to the Centre Party and interestingly only this party on the centre right remained aloof to the dramatic voting surge towards the Nazi Party.

By and large, the major electoral gains for the Nazi Party from 1930 onwards were won at the expense of the large number of right-wing special-interest parties, and by an influx of voters from the DNVP. The Nazi Party won votes from former supporters of fringe parties and in areas of Germany where they faced no major competition from traditional parties with strong local organisations and loyal support.

One of the most remarkable aspects of the Nazi breakthrough in September 1930 was that nearly a quarter of those who voted in 1930 had never voted in any previous Weimar election. A great many of these were of the older generation, who switched votes from the old conservative DNVP because they were completely disillusioned with democracy. The Nazis also did particularly well among women who voted Nazi for similar reasons. The Nazis were also successful in gaining a foothold among important middle-class occupational groups, including teachers, engineers and lawyers. The Nazi Party was extremely popular among university students, while the Hitler Youth offered young people responsibility, and helped to provide the party with many future party activists and voters.

The Nazis did gain some working-class support, but there is a danger of exaggerating it. One in every ten SPD voters switched to the Nazis compared with one in every three former conservatives and one in four former liberals. According to Jürgen Falter's computer data on Nazi voters, 40 per cent were workers, but these tended to be rural labourers and, in industrial regions, those employed in small-scale craft and domestic industries with no tradition of trade unions. Voters in large urban cities and industrial regions were generally most resistant to the appeal of Nazism, though the Nazis did win some significant increased support from industrial areas such as Saxony and the Ruhr. Such voters tended to be disillusioned former SPD supporters rather than communists and seem to have been drawn by the Nazi promise of public works programmes and restoring the position of skilled workers. By and large, the bigger and more industrial the city, the weaker was the Nazi vote. In the July 1932 national election, for instance, in German cities with a population exceeding 100,000, Nazi electoral support was 10 per cent lower than in small towns. The Nazi Party failed to win substantial support from members of trade unions. In areas with the highest concentrations of unemployed industrial workers, the KPD did best, often securing over 60 per cent of the vote.

The hard core of Nazi electoral support in the September 1930 election came from the lower-middle-class voters in rural Protestant areas, most notably, small shopkeepers, independent skilled workers, tradesmen, farmers and agricultural labourers. At the July 1932 election, the Nazis attracted new supporters such as white-collar workers, teachers, doctors, civil servants and engineers. The areas of big industrial cities in which the Nazis attracted voters were predominantly middle-class residential areas. Even so, it would be wrong to depict new Nazi Party voters after 1930 as Protestant, rural and lower-middle-class. Wage-earning manual workers and their partners made up nearly half the electorate in Weimar Germany and the SPD and KPD secured just under a third of the vote, which means significant numbers of working-class voters must have voted Nazi. A broader cross-section of the German electorate voted for the Nazi Party than for any other German political party. It was able to act as a catch-all party of mass protest which appealed to every social group in the land. It unified a group of highly disparate voters into a 'national' desire for a 'new Germany'.

THE PSYCHOLOGICAL ATTRACTION OF NAZISM TO VOTERS

Traditional accounts of Hitler's rise to power usually confine themselves to the political, economic and electoral factors, but there was something psychological going on in the minds of the German people in the later Weimar period that requires some consideration too. Historians have failed to adequately explain just what was happening to large sections of the German population between 1930 and 1933. One reason for this can be explained by the empirical and specialised nature of much historical study with its reliance on documentary sources, its fear of theory and the difficulties of quantifying public opinion. Erich Fromm has argued that social psychology provides a useful frame of reference by which the rise of Nazism can be more effectively contextualised. He emphasises that all societies are bound together by a sense of stability, combined with traditions and rituals which, if severely disrupted, can lead to a 'crisis' and a desire for a return of 'harmony' and 'stability' and 'order'. According to Fromm, in the crisis that befell Germany in the early 1930s Nazism came to be seen by millions of Germans as the best way out of an uncontrollable situation.

Germany had certainly entered a profound crisis after 1930, in which democracy was seen as totally incapable of restoring a united collective national identity. By July 1932, almost 13 million Germans felt the Nazi Party offered the best way out of chaos and they were willing to allow Hitler to create a 'National Community'. The Nazi emphasis on the strong leader, the symbols, the posters, the torchlight parades, the uniforms, the mass rallies, and the emotional speeches of Hitler all combined to win over millions of Germans. Michael Burleigh suggests the appeal of Nazism to some Germans represented a desire to belong to a secular religious movement. This view is problematic. Nazism was not complex enough to become a religion, but Burleigh's recent interpretation does highlight the need for historians to appreciate the deeper psychological appeal of Nazism in order to fully understand why Hitler came to power and the horrors that ensued.

The political and economic crisis in Germany in the early 1930s was deep-seated. Normality was first of all disrupted by the 'Great Inflation', and then shattered by the 'Great Depression'. No German democratic government brought stability or order. Bitter street violence added to a growing feeling, especially among the normally stable middle class, that 'something must be done'. The desire to 'restore order' grew within the old conservative clique surrounding Hindenburg too – but they were afraid of bringing Hitler to power, at least initially.

7

Hitler's Intriguing Road to Power, 1930–1933

THE BRÜNING EXPERIMENT, 1930–1932

The surge of support for the Nazis at the 1930 elections dealt a severe blow to hopes of Heinrich Brüning, of the Catholic Centre Party, establishing a right-wing 'national government'. The dire state of the German economy meant public spending cuts would be introduced whoever ruled. Brüning required the toleration of the Social Democrats to support his austerity measures. The SPD only agreed in order to ward off Nazi Party involvement in his government, but Adolf Hitler adopted an 'All or Nothing' strategy. This meant he would only become Chancellor, ruling under Article 48 of the constitution. Hindenburg saw that as too much of a risk and wanted to keep the Nazi leader at a distance.

Brüning's two years in power proved utterly disastrous for the economy and the credibility of democratic government. Brüning later claimed that restoring the German monarchy had been his chief aim, but it was his deflationary economic policies that led to his downfall. He was an expert on financial matters and introduced a bleak set of austerity measures including public expenditure cuts, salary reductions for public sector workers, tax increases and huge reductions in health and unemployment benefits. He ruled out borrowing to meet government expenditure or printing money. This strong medicine designed to make Germans live within their means simply decreased consumer spending, brought banks close to collapse, increased unemployment to a staggering 6 million and reduced wages to 1927 levels. It was hurting, but not working.

Brüning reduced the power and influence of the Reichstag too. It sat for just 94 days in 1930, 42 in 1931 and a measly 13 in 1932. Instead of consulting parliament, he ruled by a series of presidential decrees and grew increasingly dependent on the small coterie of power brokers surrounding Hindenburg. Tough new curbs on the freedom of the press were introduced that compromised freedom of speech, which is vital in a healthy democracy. Brüning was not exactly a dictator, but a rather repressive, charmless and austere tax inspector. Cartoons in the communist press likened him to the mass murderer Fritz Haarmann, who chopped up the bodies of the victims.

One figure who grew to influence the ageing President – as Brüning's popularity plummeted – was Kurt von Schleicher, a lieutenant general in the army, close friend of Hindenburg's son Oskar and right-hand man of General Groener, the Defence Minister. Schleicher was a veritable king of office politics, but with political ambitions of his own. He had played a key role in influencing Hindenburg to appoint Brüning in the first place. He now hit on a plan to have Hindenburg's term as President extended, without the need for an election. Hindenburg called Adolf Hitler to a meeting in the autumn of 1931 to discuss whether he would support the proposal. In a frosty first meeting between the two men, Hitler indulged in a long tirade against democracy which left the old war hero in no doubt he would not support his idea. Hindenburg felt ill at ease with Hitler, whom he described as a 'Bohemian corporal', and he confided to Schleicher that he could never make such an 'unpredictable figure' Chancellor. A second attempt was made by Brüning to persuade Hitler to prolong Hindenburg's term in office. On 12 January 1932, Hitler sent a letter to Hindenburg stating that Brüning's proposal was 'unconstitutional' and he could not go along with it.

HITLER COURTS BIG BUSINESS AND THE ARMY

The fact that Hitler was involved in such high profile discussions shows how much his national standing rose after the electoral breakthrough of 1930. Ever since that time Hitler had fastidiously built up his connections with business and the army – two groups he felt were vital in his 'legal path' to power. 'In the summer of 1931', Otto Dietrich, Hitler's press chief noted, 'The Führer suddenly decided to concentrate systematically on cultivating industrial magnates (Shirer, 1961: 181). In January 1932, Hitler told the influential Industry Club in Dusseldorf that business had nothing to fear from a Nazi regime. The extent of big business's support in Hitler's rise to power has always been shrouded in mystery. Walter Funk claimed at the Nuremberg trial that Hitler held a series of meetings with leading business figures in the latter half of 1931, most notably Emil Kirdorf, a union-hating coal baron, the steel maker Albert Vögler and Fritz Thyseen, the head of a steel trust who gave the Nazis a gift of 100,000 gold marks and later wrote a bitter memoir called 'I paid Hitler'. Other company directors, notably, Georg von Shnitzler of IG Farben, the giant chemical company, made donations. In spite of this important financial backing, business donations were not substantial. Many leading German companies such as the electric giant Siemens and Krupp, a key arms manufacturer, gave no support. The financial accounts of the Nazi Party show membership dues made up the overwhelming basis of its funding. Big business gave the bulk of its financial support to traditional centre right parties.

Hitler went on a second charm offensive between 1930 and 1933 to assure the army its role would be enhanced by a Nazi regime. In several speeches Hitler stressed the SA posed no threat to the army's role within the state and he would only seek power by constitutional means. Leading army figures remained unconvinced Hitler could control the rowdy Stormtroopers, if offered power. In 1927, the army had forbidden recruitment of Nazi members into its ranks, but there were several high profile cases of young officers who breached this rule. Older officers, schooled in the stern 'old conservative' Prussian tradition viewed Hitler as a lower-middle-class populist and were generally aloof from Nazism. The army was not working to engineer a Hitler regime between 1930 and 1933. In the words of General Groener: 'The Nazis are greedy for power. They therefore woo the Wehrmacht, in order to use it for the political aims of their party' (Shirer, 1961: 176). In a directive sent to army officers in 1931, Groener wrote: 'Not a brick can be moved any more in the political process in Germany without the word of the army being thrown decisively in the scales' (Evans, 2003: 248). The army threw all its weight after 1931 into protecting itself from government spending cuts – and it was successful in this endeavour. Army leaders hoped an authoritarian right-wing regime could be formed that left Hitler and his Nazis out in the cold.

HITLER BIDS FOR THE PRESIDENCY, 1932

In the spring of 1932, Hitler faced the biggest decision of his political life: should he challenge Hindenburg in the Presidential Election? To run would be to challenge a legendary figure who had the power to make him Chancellor, but not to stand was an admission that National Socialism was not the ideology to rescue the German nation. On 15 February, Hindenburg announced he would seek another seven years in office. Germany had moved so far to the right by this time that Hindenburg, a Protestant, militarist and a monarchist could count on support from the socialists, trade unionists, liberals, the Centre Party and the middle-class parties. Hitler, who did not become a German citizen until 25 February 1932, a lower middle-class Austrian, former artist, corporal in the army, convict, relied on the votes of the majority of middle-class Protestants, pro-Monarchists and conservatives. Hitler was unquestionably the candidate of the right. The left felt only by re-electing the conservative President could they 'stop Hitler'. No one doubted Hindenburg would win. The only question was – how many votes would Hitler gain? A large vote would increase his credibility as a potential Chancellor greatly. In the final ballot on 10 April 1932, Hindenburg took 53 per cent (amounting to 19.3 million votes); Hitler 36.8 per cent (13.4 million); and the Communist leader, Ernst Thaelmann 10.2 per cent (3.7 million). The anti-democratic Hindenburg was affirmed as the most popular political figure in Germany, but nearly all of his votes came from voters who supported parties of the centre left. Adolf Hitler won the votes of supporters of the centre right. Hitler had fought an ultra-modern campaign called 'Hitler over Germany' that focused on his personality and he flew to 46 towns and cities in a rented aircraft. Hindenburg had won, but with the wrong voters. Hitler was now the most popular civilian politician in Germany – a clear potential Chancellor.

FRANZ VON PAPEN: A NAZI IN A PIN-STRIPED SUIT?

After Hitler's defeat, rumours spread in the press that the SA was planning a Nazi *coup d'etat*. On 14 May 1932, Brüning decided to ban Hitler's SA – led by Ernst Roehm. This was a bitter blow to the Nazis as these street thugs were vital in fomenting the idea of violence on the streets. Schleicher, who opposed the ban, opened talks with Roehm and Hindenburg to try and get the ban lifted. In the first week of May, Goebbels predicted in his diary: 'Hitler has a decisive conference with General Schleicher, and with some gentlemen close to the President. Everything goes well. Brüning will fall in a few days' (Shirer, 1961: 203). On 10 May, General Groener gave a speech in the Reichstag defending the ban on the SA, but he was noisily shouted down by Nazi deputies and he resigned the next day. Brüning offered the post of Minister of Defence to General Schleicher. 'I will take it', he replied, 'but not in your government.' On 29 May 1932, Hindenburg summoned Brüning to his office and told him his position was now untenable. The following day he resigned too.

The fall of Brüning, who had tried to stand up to Hitler's street-fighting SA, emphasised toleration of the Nazis was growing at the top of the German state. On 8 May, Hindenburg met Adolf Hitler and offered him a deal: if the ban on the SA was lifted, and new elections called, would Hitler support a 'Presidential Cabinet' chosen by Hindenburg? Hitler, realising the Nazi Party stood to make substantial gains in the election, said yes. On 1 June, Hindenburg appointed Franz von Papen as Chancellor, on the recommendation of Schleicher who felt he would be sympathetic to the interests of the army. Papen, a former army officer and wealthy industrialist, was a nationalist aligned with the Centre Party, but not supported by it. He did not even have a seat in the Reichstag. Hindenburg advised Papen to form a national govern-ment standing 'above the political parties' and the Reichstag. The press called it 'the Cabinet of Barons', as it contained five members of the aristocracy. Papen earned the nickname 'The Nazi in a pin-striped suit' from the left. In hindsight, Papen's appointment was the real end of democracy in Weimar Germany, a full eight months before Hitler came to power.

Papen moved Germany sharply to the far right. He announced policies on German national radio, not in the Reichstag. He held elaborate military parades in Berlin. His greatest desire was to persuade Hitler to support his new regime. On 4 June he announced new elections, set for 31 July, fully realising Nazi support was likely to increase dramatically. On 15 June, he rashly lifted the ban on Hitler's SA – part of a shady deal Schleicher had brokered prior to the fall of Brüning. A brutal wave of street violence and rioting now erupted between Nazis and communists. In the first three weeks of June, there were 461 pitched street battles in Prussia alone, resulting in 82 deaths, hundreds of injuries, looting and property damage. In July, 38 Nazis and 30 Communists were listed among 86 victims of street riots. Law and order was clearly breaking down. Panic gripped the public. The foreign press reported that Germany was on the brink of civil war. Papen tried to restore order with a range of repressive measures. He banned all political paramilitary parades during the election campaign.

On 20 July, Papen dismissed the democratically elected Prussian government, the last major state legislature controlled by the SPD and appointed himself as 'Reich Commissioner for Prussia', with sweeping dictatorial 'emergency' powers. The new Papen Prussian government purged the civil service of Catholics, Jews and socialists. This was a very significant move towards creat-ing an authoritarian regime for the whole of Germany, as Prussia covered over half the territory of the Reich. To quell the street riots, Papen declared 'Martial Law' in Berlin and ordered police chiefs throughout Germany to arrest known rioters – but this was interpreted locally as a green light to round up communists.

THE JULY 1932 ELECTION AND ITS AFTERMATH

It was in this exceptionally feverish and violent atmosphere that Germans went to the polls on 31 July 1932. Goebbels orchestrated a propaganda blitz which consisted of posters, rallies, banners, and flags. Hitler flew from city to city on a nationwide speaking tour. He ranted against the Weimar

Republic with its warring parties, promised an end to the 'Red Menace' on the streets and a new Germany that would restore German pride. A memorable Nazi poster summed up the campaign in one slogan: 'Hitler – Germany's Last Chance'.

The July 1932 election was Hitler's greatest triumph in the Weimar era. The Nazi Party doubled its vote from 6.4 million to a massive 13.8 million votes, representing 37.4 per cent of the electorate and 230 seats in the Reichstag. This put the party nearly a hundred seats ahead of the SPD on 133. The Nazi Party had assumed the title of most popular party in Germany. If a British first-past-the post system had been in operation Hitler would have won an overall majority of seats. The Communist KPD increased its seats from 77 to 89 seats. The Centre Party went up slightly to 75 seats. The DNVP was reduced to only 37 seats and the liberal parties lost a combined total of 51 seats. The reasons for the Nazi success in July 1932 were much the same as September 1930, as the economic and political crisis had grown much worse. The new factor in 1932 was the way in which traditional middle-class voters such as teachers, civil servants, lawyers, engineers, small businessmen had switched their allegiance from conservative and liberal parties to the Nazis, especially in the affluent suburbs of big cities. Hitler had united the entire centre right of German politics. Only the Centre Party, supported by Catholic Germany, survived this onslaught, but this party had moved sharply to the right in any case. Overall, the SPD and KPD – representing the working class – polled 13.3 million in total, against 13.7 for the Nazis, with all remaining parties polling 9.8 million.

In spite of this stunning leap in Nazi Party support Hitler continued to rule out joining a coalition government and insisted he would only become Chancellor in a Nazi government, given full power to rule using Article 48 of the constitution. On 13 August 1932, Hitler met Hindenburg and demanded to be made Chancellor on his terms. All Hindenburg offered him was a place in the Cabinet. Hitler turned him down. After the meeting Hitler told his supporters: 'German racial comrades! Anyone among you who possess any feeling for the nation's honour and freedom will understand why I will not enter this government . . . I want victory for a nationalistic Germany and annihilation for its Marxist destroyers and corrupters' (Evans, 2003: 297). The refusal of Hindenburg to appoint Hitler as Chancellor was a very serious blow. Goebbels, writing in his diary at this time, felt the Nazi Party, in a proportional representation system, was unlikely to win an overall majority of voters and only through a coalition could the Nazis gain power.

Papen decided the increase in the Nazi vote was a green light to destroy democracy. Hindenburg did not want to go back to a parliamentary system of rule. Papen felt the best way forward was to create a 'Presidential Dictatorship', with Hindenburg ruling under Article 48, and publicly declaring there would be no more democratic elections. This idea was leaked by Schleicher to the Nazis. When Papen went before the Reichstag to request dissolution of parliament he was shouted down. Hermann Goering, the chairman, accepted a Communist motion for a vote of no-confidence. It was carried by 512 to 42. It was utter humiliation for Papen, illustrating he had no parliamentary support at all. Papen was left with no alternative, but to call another election on 6 November 1932.

The results showed the Nazi Party vote had seemingly peaked. Voters were clearly dismayed by Hitler's refusal to join the Papen government. The Nazi vote fell from 13.7 million to 11.7 million and its seats from 230 to 196. The Communists went up to 100 seats – a gain of 11 and 750,000 votes. The DNVP went up from 37 to 51 seats, but the SPD lost another 12 seats. Complicated negotiations followed among Hindenburg's 'inner circle' about what to do next. Hitler was in a much weaker position to bargain for power than he had been in July. He was beginning to look like an irresponsible politician who baulked at the responsibility of high office. Gregor Strasser, the chief party organiser, believed Hitler's intransigent 'All or Nothing' policy of refusing to join any coalition was leading the party down a blind alley. The Nazi Party, which relied on members' subscriptions, had exhausted its funds fighting the Presidential Election and two national elections in one year.

In practice, the supposedly democratic Weimar constitution was no different from what it had been under Bismarck in the 1870s, with each government appointed by the head of state and the Reichstag politically insignificant. Hindenburg had turned into the Kaiser. Papen was told by Schleicher the army could no longer give him support and he resigned on 17 November 1932. Hitler was invited to meet the President two days later. At this meeting, Hindenburg offered Hitler the Chancellorship on condition he could gain a majority in the Reichstag, or alternatively the post of Vice Chancellor under Papen, in a Cabinet chosen by the President. The Centre Party agreed to support Hitler, but only on the strict condition he did not immediately set up a dictatorship. Hugenberg, the DNVP leader, refused to offer support. Hitler met Hindenburg on 21 November to tell him he could not obtain a workable majority in the Reichstag, and once again demanded to rule as Chancellor under Article 48. Hindenburg told Hitler if he gave him power under emergency decree he felt such a government would swiftly turn into a dictatorship. He could only offer him Vice Chancellor under Papen. Hitler turn this down. These meetings show that Hindenburg still remained unsure about placing the fate of Germany in the hands of Adolf Hitler. There were many others in Hindenburg's circle, most notably, Papen, who believed Hitler could be 'tamed' or 'domesticated' once given the awesome responsibility of office.

GENERAL VON SCHLEICHER'S
FIFTY-SEVEN DAYS IN OFFICE

Papen now felt the way was open for him to return as Chancellor. He had clearly not reckoned with the endless scheming of Schleicher who hit on the bizarre idea of creating a centre left coalition, involving the 'socialist' wing of the Nazi Party and the SPD. He opened negotiations with Gregor Strasser, the leading 'socialist' Nazi and offered him the post of Vice Chancellor in such a government. Totally unaware of this plan, Papen, accompanied by Schleicher, held a meeting with Hindenburg on 1 December. Papen suggested he should be appointed Chancellor, then keep the Reichstag in abeyance by calling a 'state of emergency' and amend the constitution. In effect, Papen wanted Hindenburg to allow him to set up a dictatorship. Schleicher suddenly objected to this proposal and claimed he could put together a coalition government that could command a majority in the Reichstag. Hindenburg rejected this idea. The meeting ended by Hindenburg telling Papen to form a new government, but with little clarity over whether he had agreed to set in motion plans for a Papen-led dictatorship. On the following morning, Papen held a Cabinet meeting. Out of nowhere, Schleicher tabled a report, written by Major Eugen Ott, which claimed the army could not keep order against both the Communists and the Nazis in the event of a 'state of emergency' being declared and advising a coalition government was the best option. Papen, grasping that Schleicher had conspired against him, promptly adjourned the meeting and hurried off to see Hindenburg. He urged the President to sack Schleicher as Minister of Defence forthwith, but Hindenburg told him that, 'Our only hope is to let Schleicher try his luck' (Shirer, 1961: 220).

Hindenburg appointed Schleicher as Chancellor later the same day. He was the first General to occupy the post since 1890. This was an act of supreme desperation by the old and frail Hindenburg. In his diary entry for 2 December 1932, Goebbels confidently predicted: 'He [Schleicher] won't last long'. 'I was in power only fifty-seven days', Schleicher later commented, 'and on each one of them I was betrayed fifty-seven times. Don't ever speak to me about German loyalty!' (Shirer, 1961: 221). Schleicher, the master of backstage conspiracies and the negative word in the ear, was forced out into the public gaze and proved out of his depth. Papen, seething with anger, was determined to exact revenge for his humiliating exit sooner rather than later.

Schleicher announced the main task of the new government was to tackle unemployment. He opened talks with Gregor Strasser about the possibility of becoming Vice Chancellor, in the hope of splitting the Nazi

Party. This came to nothing. Strasser was forced to flee to Italy in fear of his life and resigned from all his offices in the Nazi Party. In his diary on 9 December 1932, Goebbels described him as 'A dead man'. This was an accurate prophecy. He was murdered in 1934 when Hitler exacted revenge on a number of his opponents during the 'Night of the Long Knives'.

HITLER COMES TO POWER, JANUARY 1933

It was Papen who played the decisive role in persuading Hindenburg to bring Hitler to power. Papen now opened secret talks with Hitler during December 1932 and January 1933 and concluded Hitler could be harnessed to serve the needs of the conservative old guard. By now, Hitler realised his 'All or Nothing' strategy would not bring him to power and so he had to show tactical flexibility in search of his ultimate goal. This could only be achieved through a coalition brokered by the wily Papen. On 22 January 1933, a decisive meeting took place, at the Berlin home of a rising young Nazi called Joachim von Ribbentrop, between Hindenburg's son Oskar, who had previously opposed the Nazis coming to power, and Adolf Hitler. The President's son was impressed by the Nazi leader and told an aide: 'The Nazis have to be brought into government' (Shirer, 1961: 228). It was the conversion of his trusted son that was vital in changing Hindenburg's mind too on the issue of appointing Hitler Chancellor.

On 23 January, Schleicher having failed to find a majority in the Reichstag met Hindenburg and asked him for permission to transform his government into a military dictatorship. Hindenburg told Schleicher bluntly – find a Reichstag majority or resign. This was impossible and so he resigned on 28 January. All Schleicher had succeeded in doing as Chancellor was to make a Hitler-led government seem a more palatable option. Hindenburg now told Papen to explore the possibility of forming a 'national coalition', with Hitler as Chancellor 'within the terms of the constitution'.

On the the freezing cold morning of 30 January 1933 Hindenburg appointed Adolf Hitler Chancellor of a coalition government, with Papen as Vice Chancellor, and including Hugenberg, the DNVP leader. The Cabinet only contained three Nazis, Hitler, Wilhelm Frick as Minister of the Interior, and Hermann Goering, as Minister without portfolio. The other Cabinet posts went to members of the conservative old guard. Hindenburg gave Hitler the opportunity to establish a stable and popular right-wing authoritarian government, but one that upheld the aims of the army, the agrarian Junkers, and big business, not the ideals of the Nazi Party. Papen felt the inexperienced new Chancellor could be controlled. 'We've engaged him for ourselves', he told a conservative colleague. 'Within two months we will have pushed Hitler so far into a corner that he'll squeak'. As Germany and the rest of the world would soon discover, this mouse roared. A National Socialist dictatorship was established within a space of five months in 1933. Following the death of Hindenburg – the undertaker of Weimar democracy – in August 1934, Hitler had created a personal dictatorship over Germany based on Nazi ideals.

Part 3

ASSESSMENT

8

Why did Hitler Come to Power?

It might seem logical to conclude that Hitler could only have made his way to power through the back door, but the reasons are more complex and have been the subject of intense historical debate. Most studies of the collapse of democracy in Germany always concentrate on the following factors: the vulnerability of the Weimar constitution, the problems created by the imposition of the Versailles Treaty, the impact of economic difficulties, most notably the 'great inflation' and the economic slump of the early 1930s, the lack of a democratic consensus, and the existence of extreme parties of the left and right who desired the overthrow of democracy.

With such a long list of seemingly insoluble problems it is surprising the Weimar Republic lasted so long. Yet we need to remember it survived longer than Hitler's Third Reich. All the 'factors' that led to the rise of Hitler did not occur simultaneously. The period from 1918 to 1923 was politically and economically unstable, but democracy weathered the various assaults from right and left. Between 1924 and 1929 democratic rule was never once seriously threatened and the economy started to show signs of recovery. Even in the crisis period after 1930 no attempt was made to overthrow the republic by force.

The commonly held view that the 'Great Depression' brought Hitler to power is not credible either. The USA suffered economic problems as difficult as Germany, but fascism did not emerge there. There was something specific about the nature of the crisis in Germany that was as much political and psychological as purely economic. The decision of President Hindenburg to bypass the Reichstag between 1930 and 1933 and choose his own hand-picked leaders, all of whom had no popular authority, deepened the political crisis and undermined the legitimacy of democratic government. German voters didn't seem to mind and voted for extreme parties on the right and left.

The really decisive ingredients in the period 1930 to 1933 were the supreme indifference of Hindenburg and his inner circle to sustain democracy, and the growth in support for Adolf Hitler and the Nazi Party. It was the mixture of these two factors, operating at a time of deep economic depression, which ensured the collapse of Weimar democracy.

Some historians would go further and pin all the blame on the old 'conservative' authoritarian right who brought Adolf Hitler to power, having exhausted all the other alternatives, in the hope he could be tamed, and used to serve their own authoritarian interests. By using Article 48 to sustain unrepresentative leaders from 1930 onwards, Hindenburg mortally damaged the infant democratic structure in Weimar Germany and paved the way to authoritarian dictatorship during the 1930s. It was not the constitution of Weimar or even its voting system that was flawed. It was the actions of those personalities given the responsibility to uphold it who must take the blame. According to Alan Bullock – and many other historians – Hitler was 'jobbed into office' at a time when the electoral popularity of the Nazi Party was on the wane (Bullock, 1962). Some left-wing historians went further, depicting Hitler as the 'unwitting agent' of the bourgeoisie, serving much the same function as Napoleon had done for the bourgeoisie during the French Revolution. For Georgi Dimitroff, Nazism was the 'open terrorist dictatorship of the most reactionary, most chauvinist and most imperial elements of finance capital' (Kershaw, 2000: 12). The major problem in viewing Hitler as the 'pawn' of the upper classes or a 'puppet of big business' is that this reduces the hugely important role Hitler's personality and political skills exerted on events. The desire to reduce Hitler and Nazism to mere deterministic symptom of a deep crisis within capitalism has fallen, much as the Berlin Wall did in 1989.

We must not forget that from 1930 onwards Adolf Hitler was undoubtedly the single most dynamic politician in German politics. By July 1932, the Nazi Party was supported by nearly 13 million German people of voting age. As we have seen, new research on voting behaviour is revealing that the Nazi Party drew support from a broader range of class groupings than any other German party. The key reason these diverse groups supported Nazism was not primarily because of its opposition to the Treaty of Versailles or anti-Semitism, but was more due to Hitler's powerful utopian promise to end class-based politics, and replace them with a popular ethnically united folk community. A great part of this appeal, especially to the middle classes, but also to working-class supporters of Nazism as well, was a desire to weaken the power of Marxism and democratic government, which an increasing majority of Germans felt could not provide stability or hope. It was the mass popular electoral support of Hitler's ideas to millions of Germans that was the decisive factor as to why he was in a position to be offered power in 1933.

Of course, there are dangers in stressing the 'uniqueness' of Nazism and the 'peculiarities' of German history, but there were some very distinctive aspects in German politics, culture and society in the Weimar era that allowed nation-alism to survive and then flourish. Defeat in the 'Great War' was never really overcome by a large proportion of the population. Feelings of humiliation, frustration, bitterness, insecurity and anger festered across the political spectrum, but especially among the solid middle-class groups that offer stability to long lasting democratic nations. This upheaval occurred at a time of great changes within modern industrial societies. Countries without long democratic traditions such as Germany, Italy and Russia all lapsed into authoritarianism during the inter-war years, while Britain, France and the USA – all victorious powers – retained their democracies and expanded their voting systems to cover the entire population.

It is still difficult to determine whether the rise of the Nazi Party was the public expression of an irrational and incomprehensible resistance to 'modernisation', an 'Escape from Freedom' or a specific German response to the imposition of a modern democracy in a society whose recent history had been characterised by authoritarian rule. Ernst Notle argues that Nazism was more a reaction to the fear of the spread of Marxism than anything else and that fear was at its height in the Weimar era. The presence among the hard-core supporters of Nazism of so many passionate opponents of Marxism gives such a view some credence. In rural small areas many Nazi voters felt industrial workers were getting a better deal than farmers and agricultural workers. In the big cities, the middle classes felt their living standards were being eroded by increased taxes that were used to finance social welfare payments for 'the workers'. Detlev Peukert argues that the rise of the Nazi Party combined traditional 'conservative' values such as the promise to restore an authoritarian system of government, and a return to the land, with a desire to use modern techniques in industry for the good of the 'nation' through rearmament and promised a more efficient use of industrial resources for the good of the whole nation not just one powerful segment of it – the industrial working class (Fischer, 1995: 123).

George Mosse views Nazism as a unique revolution of the right, with goals of its own, not a mere opportunistic movement led by a power-crazed individual without any clear ideological objectives (Mosse, 1966). According to Roger Griffin, Nazism was not the agent of any other force, or the reflection of one single class, but was the product of the conditions which existed in countries with powerful nationalist forces and limited experience of democratic traditions. It was not an attempt to stop modernisation by simply 'turning back the clock', but promised to use modern ideas and traditional values to create a new utopia, a genuine third way between liberal democracy and socialism. Ian Kershaw suggests research on the social basis of Nazi electoral support before 1933 strongly suggested it was the dynamic and radical aspects of the Nazi programme and its support for 'modernisation' which attracted new voters as much as the backward-looking, often anti-scientific, negative and reactionary aspects of its electoral propaganda (Kershaw, 2000).

Hitler never supported the de-industrialisation ideas of sections of the most extreme right of the party. Central to the Nazi appeal to voters was Hitler's promise to place strong industrial and agricultural sectors in the service of national unity.

Hitler offered this utopian vision at a time of deep gloom and pessimism. It clearly struck a deep chord with millions of voters. Hitler tried to come to power with the support of voters and collaborated with existing elites to achieve power as a necessary evil, but he was opposed to coalition government and he never wavered from his view that the Nazi Party would use power to destroy democracy and that was a promise he kept. To achieve this 'National Socialist Revolution' he promised severe and brutal measures would be essential and never hid his intentions in his public speeches. Even though Hitler's proposed utopia was unrealisable it struck a deep chord with many sections of German society during the economic downturn after 1929.

The reason why Nazism grew so rapidly after 1929 was that millions of Germans felt democratic government, a relatively new phenomenon in Germany, had been a monumental failure. The Nazi Party promised not just to rid Germany of democracy, but promised a new beginning for Germany and also a restoration of some of the values many in the middle classes felt had been eroded since 1918. Another factor, which unquestionably attracted voters to the Nazi Party, was the promise by Hitler to deal with the 'red menace' on the streets. In their street fights with communists the Nazis depicted themselves as the 'defenders of the German people', while Nazi Party propaganda played up the idea that Hitler was not only the best insurance against a communist revolution, but that he would use the power of the state to restore law and order by clamping down on the rights and freedoms enjoyed by the left.

What Hitler offered, above all, was the simple promise of strong and clear leadership based on authoritarian principles. Many Germans who turned to the Nazis found the idea of a strong leader determined to restore order very appealing. We should remember that Hitler was a charismatic public speaker who spoke with a passion many describe in almost religious terms [**Doc. 18, p. 124**]. We may not be able to comprehend Hitler's power to inspire at this place and time, and given what came later, we may not wish to believe it ever existed. Yet to deny it existed, or to dismiss Hitler's seductive power to rouse many millions of Germans is a dereliction of analytical objectivity.

Hitler's political ability should not be underestimated either. He turned the Nazi Party into a modern party with brilliant electioneering tactics. He was able to occupy the political vacuum of the right of German politics and by 1932 he was the only civilian politician who stood any chance of establishing a popular authoritarian regime. The only alternatives to Hitler coming to power by then were a presidential dictatorship led by the old and increasingly frail Hindenburg or an authoritarian regime chosen by the President, but his choice of deeply unpopular individuals such as Brüning, Papen and Schleicher made Hitler seem an even more attractive option to German voters. Hindenburg continued to look for a politician he could control, and eventually Papen persuaded him it was worth risking Hitler in the hope he could be shackled, controlled and then utilised to serve 'the old guard'. This was a monumental error of political judgement and a severe underestimation of Hitler's determination to destroy the constitution and set up a dictatorship soon after he was given office.

Hitler did not destroy democracy in Germany. Hindenburg had already done that progressively between 1930 and 1933 by deciding to rule by emergency decrees with little reference to the Reichstag or the will of the voters. This simply played into Hitler's hands, as each Hindenburg-appointed Chancellor proved incapable of ruling effectively for very long. The German people played their part too. Without the dramatic surge of popular support for the Nazi Party between 1930 and 1933 Hitler would not have been in the position to bargain for power in the first place.

The constant horse-trading and compromises necessary to maintain a viable government during a period of deep-seated political and economic crisis, with violence raging out on the streets, sapped the energy of Hindenburg and left the voters in despair. A vote in elections counted for nothing after 1930. Hindenburg had reduced democracy to a complete sham. The backbone of any democracy is strong political parties determined to uphold the existing system, supported by the vast majority of voters and the forces of law and order. In Germany, such a situation did not exist. It was becoming inevitable that Hitler would be given his chance to govern once he showed some willingness to form a coalition government. Hitler was Germany's inevitable fate and also its misfortune.

Part 4

DOCUMENTS

Document 1   HITLER IN VIENNA

One of Hitler's closest friends as a young person was August Kubizek who spent some time in Vienna with the future Nazi dictator. In this document, Kubizek offers some observations on Hitler's views of the ethnic diversity of Viennese life.

When home-going workers passed us by, Adolf would grip my arm and say 'Did you hear, Gustl? Czechs!'. Another time, we encountered some bricklayers speaking loudly in Italian, with florid gestures. 'There you have your German Vienna', he cried, indignantly. This, too, was one of his oft repeated phrases: 'German Vienna', but Adolf pronounced it with a bitter undertone . . . He hated the babel in the streets of Vienna, this 'incest incarnate' as he called it later. He hated this State, which ruined Germanism, and the pillars that supported this State: the reigning house, the Church, the nobility, the capitalists and the Jews . . . His accumulated hatred of all forces which threatened the Germans was mainly concentrated upon the Jews, who played a leading role in Vienna.

Source: Kubizek, A., *Young Hitler. The Story of our Friendship*, London: Macmillan, 1954, pp. 185–186.

Document 2   HITLER'S FIRST APPEARANCE AT A MEETING OF THE GERMAN WORKERS' PARTY

In the following document, Anton Drexler, the leader of the German Workers' Party (DAP), describes his first impression of Adolf Hitler, at a party meeting.

On 12 September 1919, the German Workers' Party held a monthly meeting in the Veterans' Hall of the Sterneckerbrau . . . The first National Socialist pamphlet, My Political Awakening . . . had just appeared. I had collected a few proof copies from my publisher, Dr. Boepple, and was standing with five copies in my hand at the bar of the pub, listening with growing enthusiasm to the second speaker in the evening's discussion, who was a guest. He was dealing with the first speaker in the discussion, a Professor Baumann, who had urged the secession of Bavaria from Germany, and he was tackling the Professor in a way that was a joy to watch. He gave a short but trenchant speech in favour of a greater Germany which thrilled me and all who could hear him. When the speaker finished I rushed towards him, thanked him for what he had said and asked him to take the pamphlet I had away with him to read. It contained, I said, the rules and basic ideas of the new movement; if he was in agreement with them, he could come again in a week's time and work in a smaller circle, because we could do with people like him.

Source: Noakes, J. and Pridham, G., *Nazism 1919–1945. Vol. 1: The Rise to Power, 1919–1934*, Exeter: University of Exeter Press, 1983, p. 11.

THE TWENTY-FIVE POINTS OF THE NAZI PARTY PROGRAMME   **Document 3**

The Nazi Party programme, announced on 25 February 1920, remained the key rallying point for party members before 1933.

1. We demand the union of all Germans to form a Greater Germany on the basis of the right of self-determination enjoyed by nations.
2. We demand equality of rights for the German people in its dealings with other nations and abolition of the peace treaties of Versailles and Saint Germain.
3. We demand land and territory (colonies) for the nourishment of our people and for settling our excess population.
4. None but members of the nation may be citizens of the state. None but those of German blood, whatever their creed, may be members of the nation. No Jew therefore may be a member of the nation.
5. Anyone who is not a citizen of the state may live in Germany only as a guest and must be regarded as being subject to foreign laws.
6. The right of voting on the leadership and legislation is to be enjoyed by the state alone. We demand therefore that all official appointments, of whatever kind, whether in the Reich, in the country, or in the smaller localities, shall be granted to citizens of the state alone. We oppose Parliament's corrupting custom of filling posts merely with a view to party considerations and without reference to character or capacity.
7. We demand that the state shall make it its first duty to promote the industry and livelihood of citizens of the state. If it is not possible to nourish the entire population of the state, foreign nationals (noncitizens of the state) must be excluded from the Reich.
8. All non-German immigration must be prevented.
9. All citizens of the state shall be equal as regards rights and duties.
10. It must be the first duty of each citizen of the state to work with his mind or with his body. The activities of the individual may not clash with the interests of the whole, but must proceed within the frame of the community and be for the general good.

We demand therefore:

11. Abolition of incomes unearned by work.
12. In view of the enormous sacrifice of life and property demanded of a nation by every war, personal enrichment due to a war must be regarded as a crime against the nation. We demand therefore ruthless confiscation of all war gains.
13. We demand nationalisation of all business trusts.
14. We demand that the profits from the wholesale trade shall be shared.
15. We demand extensive development of security for old age.
16. We demand creation and maintenance of a healthy middle class, immediate communisation of wholesale business premises, and their lease at a cheap rate to small traders, and that extreme consideration shall be shown to all small purveyors to the state, district authorities and smaller localities.
17. We demand land reform suitable to our national requirements.
18. We demand ruthless prosecution of those whose activities are injurious to the common interest. Sordid criminals against the nation, usurers, profiteers, etc., must be punished by death, whatever their creed or race.
19. We demand that the Roman Law, which serves the materialistic world order, shall be replaced by a legal system for all Germany.
20. With the aim of opening to every capable and industrious German the possibility of higher education and of thus obtaining advancement, the state must consider a thorough reconstruction of our national system of education.
21. The state must see to raising the standard of health in the nation by protecting mothers and infants, prohibiting child labour, increasing bodily efficiency by obligatory gymnastics and sports laid down by law, and by extensive support of clubs engaged in the bodily development of the young.
22. We demand the abolition of a paid army and formation of a national popular army.
23. We demand legal warfare against conscious political lying and its dissemination in the press. In order to facilitate creation of a German national press we demand:
    (a) that all editors and their assistants of newspapers employing the German language must be members of the nation;
    (b) that special permission from the state shall be necessary before non-German newspapers can appear. These are not necessarily printed in the German language;
    (c) that non-Germans shall be prohibited by law from participating financially in or influencing German newspapers . . . It must be forbidden to publish papers which do not promote the national welfare. We demand legal prosecution of tendencies in art and literature of a kind likely to disintegrate our life as a nation, and

the suppression of institutions which militate against the requirements mentioned above.

24. We demand liberty for all religious denominations in the state, so far as they are not a danger to it and do not militate against moral feelings of the German race. The party as such stands for positive Christianity, but does not bind itself in the matter of creed to any particular confession. It combats the Jewish-materialist spirit within us and outside us.

25. That all the foregoing may be realised, we demand the creation of a strong central power in the state. Unquestioned authority of the politically centralised Parliament over the entire Reich and its organisations and formation of chambers for classes and occupations for the purpose of carrying out the general laws promulgated by the Reich in the various states of the confederation.

The leaders of the party swear to go straight forward – if necessary, to sacrifice their lives – in securing the fulfilment of the foregoing points.

Source: Nazi Party programme (1920).

THE DEMANDS OF THE NAZI PARTY   **Document 4**

In this document, Hitler outlines some of the key demands of the Nazi Party.

1. We must call to account the November criminals of 1918. It cannot be that two million Germans should have fallen in vain and afterwards one should sit down as friends at the same table with traitors. No, we do not pardon, we demand – Vengeance!

2. The dishonouring of the nation must cease. For the betrayers of their Fatherland and informers the gallows is the proper place. Our streets and squares shall once more bear the names of our heroes; they shall not be named after Jews. In the Question of Guilt we must proclaim the truth.

3. The administration of the state must be cleared of the rabble which is fattened at the state of the parties.

4. The present laxity in the fight against usury must be abandoned. Here the punishment is the same as that for the betrayers of their Fatherland.

5. We must demand a great enlightenment on the subject of the peace treaty. With thoughts of love? No! But in holy hatred against those who have ruined us.

6. The lies which veil from us our misfortunes must cease. The fraud of the present money madness must be shown up . . .

7. As the foundation for a new currency, the property of those who are not of our blood will be used. If families who have lived in Germany for a thousand years are now expropriated, we must do the same to the Jewish usurers.

8. We demand the immediate expulsion of all Jews who have entered Germany since 1914, and all those too, who through the trickery of the stock exchange or through other shady transactions have gained their wealth.

9. The housing scarcity must be relieved through energetic action; houses must be granted to those who deserve them.

Source: Hitler speech, 18 September 1922, quoted in Baynes, N., *The Speeches of Adolf Hitler, Vol. 1*, Oxford: Oxford University Press, 1942, pp. 107–108.

Document 5   HITLER ON THE LEADERSHIP PRINCIPLE

The idea of total authority being invested in the leader of the Nazi Party was established in 1921, and became a key aspect of the organisation of the party thereafter. In this document, Adolf Hitler explains the origin of the leadership principle.

In the years 1920–21 the movement had a committee in control of it, elected by the members in assembly. This committee, comically enough, embodied the very principle which the movement was most keenly fighting, namely, parliamentarianism. I refused to countenance such folly, and after a very short time I ceased to attend the meetings of the committee. I made my propaganda as I wished, and that was the end of it . . . As soon as the new rules were adopted and I was established as Chairman of the party, thus acquiring the necessary authority and the rights accompanying it, all such folly came to an immediate end. Decisions by committee were replaced by the principle of absolute responsibility. The Chairman is responsible for entire control of the movement.

The principle gradually became recognised inside the movement as a natural one, at least as far as control of the party was concerned.

Source: Hitler, A., *Mein Kampf*, London: Paternoster, 1938, pp. 234–235.

Document 6   THE MUNICH BEER HALL PUTSCH

In this document, Herr Muller, a historian, who was in the Bürgerbraukeller, provides an eyewitness account of the Munich Beer Hall Putsch.

Herr von Kahr had spoken for half an hour. Then there was a movement at the entrance as if people were wanting to push their way in. Despite several warnings, the disturbance did not die down. Herr von Kahr had to break off speaking. Eventually, steel helmets came into sight. From this moment on, the view from my seat was rather obscured. People stood on chairs so that I didn't see Hitler until he had come fairly near along the main gangway; just before he turned to the platform. I saw him emerge between two armed soldiers in steel helmets who carried pistols next to their heads, pointing at the ceiling. They turned towards the platform. Hitler climbed on to a chair to my left . . . Thereupon Hitler called out . . . 'The National Revolution has broken out. The hall is surrounded' . . . The gentlemen did not move. The General State Commissioner [Kahr] had stepped back and stood back and stood opposite him, looking at him calmly. Then Hitler went towards the platform. What happened I could not see exactly. I heard him talk to the gentlemen and I heard the words: Everything would be over in ten minutes if the gentlemen would go with him. To my surprise, the three gentlemen [Kahr, Lossow and Seisser] went out with him immediately. . . . The general mood – I can of course only judge from my surroundings, but I think that this represented the general feeling in the hall – was still against the whole business. . . . The change came only during Hitler's second speech when he entered about ten minutes later, went to the platform and made a short speech. It was a rhetorical masterpiece. In fact, in a few sentences it totally transformed the mood of the audience. I have rarely seen anything like it . . . An hour after Hitler's first appearance, the three gentlemen [Kahr, Lossow and Seisser] came back into the hall, with Hitler and Ludendorff. They were enthusiastically received. On the platform Kahr began to speak first without being requested to and gave the speech which was printed word for word in the papers. Ludendorff without being requested to, whereas as Lossow and Seisser only spoke after repeated requests . . . If I am to depict the impression made by the gentleman on the platform, I would say Kahr was completely unmoved. His face was like a mask all evening. He was not pale or agitated, he was very serious, but spoke very composedly. I got the impression that there was a melancholy look in his eyes. But that is perhaps being subjective. Hitler, on the other hand was radiant with joy. One had the feeling that he was delighted to have succeeded in persuading Kahr to collaborate. There was in his demeanor, I would say, a kind of childhood joy, a very frank expression which I will never forget.

Source: Noakes, J. and Pridham, G., *Nazism 1919–1945. Vol. 1: The Rise to Power, 1919–1934*, Exeter: University of Exeter Press, 1983, pp. 28–29, p. 32.

HITLER ON THE KEY LESSON OF THE MUNICH BEER HALL PUTSCH   **Document 7**

In the following document, taken from a speech given by Hitler in 1936, the Nazi leader explains the importance of the failure in 1923 to the subsequent history of the Nazi Party.

From the failure of the Putsch we drew a great lesson for the future. And so only a few days after the collapse I formed a new decision; that now without any haste the conditions must be created which would exclude the possibility of another failure . . . The experience of 1923 produced later the miracle that we could effect a revolution without in the least disturbing domestic order or bringing the life of our people in danger . . . We have conquered our State without, I believe, the breaking of a single window pane. This was possible only thanks to thorough preparation and the building up of the Party . . . And the greatest miracle of all; it is perhaps due solely to the experience of 1923 that we were able to sail round the rock which faces any revolution such as ours, viz., the problem of our relation to the existing so-called 'legal instruments of power' of the state.

Source: Hitler speech, September 1936, quoted in Baynes, N., *The Speeches of Adolf Hitler, Vol. 1*, Oxford: Oxford University Press, 1942, pp. 155–158.

Document 8   JOSEPH GOEBBELS' VIEWS ON NATIONAL SOCIALISM

In this document, from the mid-1920s Joseph Goebbels outlines differences between National Socialism and Marxist and liberal nationalist parties.

There are people in our camp, not the worst ones, who learned something after 1918 and are therefore still learning after 1923. Today they see not only the falsification of the socialist idea in Marxism, but also, just as clearly and plainly, the falsification of nationalism in the so-called national parties and organisations of every hue. They are prepared to draw from these insights the necessary political conclusions. They turn just as sharply against middle-class views as against Marxist proletarian ones . . . For them, the middle class, in its political organisations, has lost the right to take a stand against any consequence of the politics of this system just as much as has Marxism, because both are guilty of this system, because both have participated in this system and will continue to do so, whenever and wherever the stampede to the fodder trough permits it. Down with the madness of Marxism, for it is falsified socialism! Down with the madness of the so-called nationalist opposition in the parties of the right! For it is falsified nationalism. These are the slogans which make socialism into nationalism and nationalism into socialism. For us any nationalist demand requires a socialist one; any radicalisation of the national will for freedom a radicalisation of socialism. You consistently confuse system and person. But is always the system itself which is in question, never its temporary supporters.

Source: Goebbels, J., 'The Radicalisation of Socialism' quoted in Lane, B. Miller and Leila, J. (eds), *Nazi Ideology Before 1933. A Documentation*, Manchester: Manchester University Press, 1978, pp. 79–80.

HITLER ON THE POWER OF THE SPOKEN WORD   **Document 9**

*In this extract, from Mein Kampf, Hitler explains the unique emotional power
of the spoken word.*

All great, world shaking events have been brought about not by written matter
but by the spoken word . . . The bourgeois intelligentsia protest against such
a view only because they themselves obviously lack the power and ability to
influence the masses by the spoken word, since they have thrown themselves
more and more into purely literary activity and renounced the real agitational
activity of the spoken word. Such habits necessarily lead in time to what distinguishes our bourgeoisie today; that is, the loss of the psychological instinct
for mass effect and mass influence.

While the speaker gets a continuous correction of his speech from the
crowd he is addressing – since he can always see in the face of his listeners to
what extent they can follow his arguments with understanding and whether
the impression and the effect of his words lead to the desired goal – the
writer does not know his readers at all. Therefore, to begin with, he will not
aim at a definite mass before his eyes but will keep his arguments entirely
general. By this to a certain degree he loses psychological subtlety and in
consequence suppleness. And so by and large a brilliant speaker will be
able to write better than a brilliant writer can speak, unless he continuously
practices this art. On top of this there is the fact that the mass of the people
as such is lazy; that they remain inertly in the spirit of their old habits and,
left to themselves, will take up a piece of written matter only reluctantly if
it is not in agreement with what they themselves believe and does not bring
them what they had hoped for. . . . The essential point, however, is that a piece
of literature never knows into what hands it will fall and yet it must retain its
definite form. In general the effect will be the greater, the more this form
corresponds to the intellectual level and nature of those very people who will
be its readers. A book that is destined for the broad masses must therefore
attempt from the very beginning to have an effect, both in style and elevation,
different from a work intended for the higher intellectual classes.

Only by this kind of adaptability does written matter approach the written
word. To my mind, the speaker can treat the same theme as the book; he will,
if he is a brilliant popular orator, not be likely to repeat the same reproach
and the same substance twice in the same form. He will always let himself
be borne by the great masses in such a way that instinctively the very words
come to his lips that he needs to speak to the hearts of his audience. And if
he errs, even in the slightest, he has the living correction before him.

As I have said, he can read from the facial expressions of his audience
whether, firstly, they understand what he is saying, whether, secondly, they
can follow the speech as a whole, and to what extent, thirdly, he has convinced them of the soundness of what he has said. If firstly he sees that they

do not understand him, he will become so primitive and clear in his explanations that even the last member of the audience has to understand him; if he feels secondly that they do not follow him, he will construct his ideas so cautiously and slowly that even the weakest member of the audience is not left behind, and he will thirdly if he suspects that they do not seem convinced of the soundness of his argument, repeat it over and over in constantly new examples. He himself will utter their objections, which he senses though unspoken, and go on contradicting them and exploding them until at length even the last group of an opposition, by its very beginning and facial expressions enables him to recognise its capitulation to his arguments.

Source: Hitler, A., *Mein Kampf, Vol. 2*, Munich: Verlag Franz Eher Nachfolger, 1927, pp. 525–536.

Document 10   THE NAZI PARTY AND PRIVATE PROPERTY

The anti-capitalist elements of the Nazi Party led to criticism from political opponents that the party would introduce 'socialist' measures if it won power. In April 1928, Hitler attempted to ease these worries by clarifying the Nazi position on private property.

In view of the false interpretations on the part of our opponents of Point 17 of the programme of the NSDAP, it is necessary to make the following statement:

Since the NSDAP accepts the principle of private property, it is self-evident that the phrase 'confiscation without compensation' refers only to the creation of possible means of confiscation, when necessary of land acquitted illegally or not managed in the public interest. It is, therefore, aimed primarily against Jewish companies which speculate on land.

Source: Noakes, J. and Pridham, G., *Nazism 1919–1945. Vol. 1: The Rise to Power, 1919–1934*, Exeter: University of Exeter Press, 1983, p. 61.

Document 11   HITLER DEBATES THE MEANING OF 'SOCIALISM' WITH OTTO STRASSER

After 1928, the Nazi Party attempted to downplay the 'socialist' parts of the party programme in order to attract votes from the middle classes and people in rural areas. Otto Strasser, and other leading radicals were alarmed by this new emphasis. The following document is taken from an interview between Strasser and Adolf Hitler in 1930 in which the issue of 'socialism' is discussed.

Hitler: 'I was once an ordinary working man. I would not allow my chauffeur to eat worse than I eat myself. But your kind of socialism is nothing but

Marxism. The mass of the working classes want nothing but bread and games. They will never understand the meaning of an ideal, and we cannot hope to win them over to one. What we have to do is to select from a new master class, men who will not allow themselves to be guided, like you, by the morality of pity. Those who rule must know they have the right to rule because they belong to a superior race. They must maintain that right and ruthlessly consolidate it . . . What you preach is liberalism, nothing but liberalism. There is only one kind of revolution, and it is not political or social, but racial, and it will always be the same: the struggle of inferior classes and races against the superior races who are in the saddle. On the day the superior race forgets this law, it is lost. All revolutions – and I have studied them carefully – have been racial . . .

Otto Strasser: 'Let us assume, Herr Hitler, that you come to power tomorrow. What would you do about Krupp's? [A leading German arms company]. Would you leave it alone or not?'

Hitler: 'Of course I would leave it alone . . . Do you think me so crazy as to want to ruin Germany's great industry?'

Otto Strasser: 'If you wish to preserve the capitalist regime, Herr Hitler, you have no right to talk of socialism. For our supporters are socialists, and your programme demands the socialisation of private enterprise.'

Hitler: 'that word 'socialism' is the trouble . . . I have never said that all enterprises should be socialised. On the contrary, I have maintained that we might socialise enterprises prejudiced to the interests of the nation. Unless they are so guilty, I should consider it a crime to destroy essential elements in our economic life. Take Italian Fascism. Our National Socialist state, like the Fascist state will safeguard both employers' and workers' interests while reserving the right of arbitration in case of dispute. There is no reason for granting the workers a share in the profits of the enterprises that employ them, and more particularly for giving them the right to be consulted . . .

Source: Noakes, J. and Pridham, G., *Nazism 1919–1945. Vol. 1: The Rise to Power, 1919–1934,* Exeter: University of Exeter Press, 1983, pp. 66–67.

HITLER DEFINES NATIONAL SOCIALISM **Document 12**

In the following document, taken from an article by Adolf Hitler in the Daily Express, published on 28 September 1930, the Nazi leader defines National Socialism.

'Nationalist' . . . I define as one to whom duty to country or community comes before self-interest; in other words, 'One for all' . . . 'Socialist' I define from the word 'social' meaning in the main 'social equity'. A Socialist is one who serves the common good without giving up his individuality . . . Our adopted term 'Socialist' has nothing to do with Marxist Socialism. Marxism is anti-property; true socialism is not. Marxism places no value on the individual or individual effort, or efficiency, true Socialism values the individual and encourages him in individual efficiency, at the same time holding that his interests as an individual must be in consonance with those of the community.'

Source: Daily Express, 28 September 1930.

Document 13   THE APPEAL OF NATIONAL SOCIALISM: A PACIFIST VIEW

In this document, Heinrich Mann, a democrat and pacifist, writing in December 1931, offers his explanation for the growth of support for the Nazi Party.

It is already evening in Germany, if not midnight. That gives Mr. Hitler his big chance, as he most likely knows. Were Germans able to examine their situation with a clear head, he would not win them over . . . The condition of Germany is above all a psychological fact. All external facts pale in comparison. The collapse of the economy would have been nothing unusual. The economy is collapsing everywhere, but only in Germany does the process achieve its maximum effect on spirits. One recalls that the currency in all countries was threatened. Only in Germany did it succumb utterly to ruin [in 1923]; the Germans let it become ruined without any external necessity, for reasons of spirit, from a deficiency of inner resistance. Thus it could be that they now allow National Socialism to come to power because they are hearing once again the call from the abyss. The Germans hear it quite frequently. The question is whether this time they will really listen to the call from the abyss. The catastrophes they have previously suffered, after all, have taught them well . . .

Speaking for the victory of National Socialism, above all, is the fact that in this country democracy has never won in bloody battle. In one historical moment, after the defeat in the war, it appeared as a possible way out, compared to the disaster of the monarchy and the threat of Bolshevism – only a way out, not a goal, much less a passionate experience . . . Now one sees that the state is treating Hitler's private army not as a threat to its own existence but as a desirable ally to increase its own power . . . Enough – these and other circumstances as well, including the power of money, speaks for the victory of National Socialism.

Source: Mann, H., 'Die deutsche Entscheidung', Das Tagebuch, vol. 12, no. 51, 19 December 1931, pp. 1964–1967.

THE NAZI APPEAL TO FARMERS   Document 14

During the early 1930s the Nazi Party enjoyed a remarkable surge of voter support from farming communities. The following document is taken from a Nazi electoral pamphlet, aimed at the German farmer, and distributed prior to the July 1932 election.

German Farmer You Belong to Hitler! Why?

The German farmer stands between two great dangers today:

The one danger is the American economic system; Big Capitalism!

it means 'world economic crisis'

it means 'eternal interest slavery'

it means that the world is nothing more than a bag of booty for Jewish finance in Wall Street, New York and Paris

it enslaves man under slogans of progress, technology, rationalisation, standardisation, etc.

it knows only profits and dividends

it wants to make the world into a giant trust

it puts machine over man

it annihilates the independent, earth-rooted farmer, and its final aim is the world dictatorship of Jewry

it achieves this in the political sphere, through parliament and the swindle of democracy. In the economic sphere, through the control of credit, the mortgaging of land, the stock exchange and the market principle.

The farmer's leagues, the Landvolk, and the Bavarian Farmers' League all pay homage to this system.

The other danger is the Marxist economic system of Bolshevism:

it knows only the state economy

it knows only one class, the proletariat

it brings in controlled economy

it doesn't just annihilate the self-sufficient farmer economically – it roots him out

it brings in the rule of the tractor

it nationalises the land and creates mammoth factory-farms

it uproots and destroys man's soul, making him the powerless tool of the communist idea – or kills him

it destroys the family, belief and customs

it is anti-Christ, it desecrates the churches

its final aim is the world dictatorship of the proletariat, that means ultimately the world dictatorship of Jewry, for the Jew controls this powerless proletariat and uses it for his dark plans

Big capitalism and bolshevism work hand in hand; they are born of Jewish thought and serve the master plan of world Jewry.

Who alone can rescue the farmer from these dangers?

NATIONAL SOCIALISM

Source: 'German Farmer You Belong to Hitler! Why?' National Socialist Pamphlet, 1932.

Document 15   A SCHOOLTEACHER DESCRIBES THE ATMOSPHERE AT A NAZI PARTY MEETING

In the following document a Hamburg schoolteacher – Luise Solmitz – describes the atmosphere at a Nazi party rally, attended by Adolf Hitler, in 1932.

Führer: Leader (Adolf Hitler). Hitler was the undisputed leader of the Nazi Party and enjoyed total power over the decision making within the Nazi Party.

The April sun shone hot like in summer and turned everything into a picture of gay expectation. There was immaculate order and discipline . . . The hours passed, the sun shone, expectations rose . . . It was nearly 3 p.m. 'The **Führer** is coming!' A ripple went through the crowds. Around the speaker's platform one could see hands raised in the Hitler salute. A speaker opened the meeting, abused the 'system', nobody listened to him. A second speaker welcomed Hitler and made way for the man who had drawn 120,000 people of all classes and ages. There stood Hitler in a simple black coat and looked over the crowd, waiting – a forest of swastika pennants were raised, the jubilation of this moment was given vent in a roaring salute. Main theme: 'Out of parties shall grow a nation, the German nation . . . Thirteen years ago I was a simple unknown soldier. I went my way. I never turned back. Nor shall I turn back now.' Otherwise he made no personal attacks, nor any promises, vague or definite.

Source: Noakes, J. and Pridham, G., *Nazism 1919–1945. Vol. 1: The Rise to Power, 1919–1934*, Exeter: University of Exeter Press, 1983, p. 74.

Document 16   HITLER'S SPEECH TO THE DUSSELDORF INDUSTRY CLUB

During 1932, Adolf Hitler attempted to cultivate support from leading figures in German industry. The following document is part of the text of Hitler's important speech to the German Industry Club in Düsseldorf on 27 January 1932.

Today we stand at the turning point of Germany's destiny. If the present development continues, Germany will one day of necessity land in Bolshevik chaos, but if this development is broken, then our people must be taken into a school of iron discipline . . . A hard schooling, but one we cannot escape!

People say to me so often: 'You are the only drummer of national Germany' And supposing that I were the only drummer? It would today be a far more statesmanlike achievement to drum once more into this German people a new faith than gradually to squander the only faith they have. Take the case of a fortress, imagine that it is reduced to extreme privations; as long as the garrison sees a possible salvation, believes in it, hopes for it, then they can bear reduced ration. But take from the hearts of men their last belief in the hope of salvation, in a better future – take that completely from them, and you will see how these men suddenly regard reduced rations as the most important thing in life.

. . . I know quite well, gentlemen, that when National Socialists march through the streets and suddenly in the evening a tumult and commotion arises, then the bourgeoisie draws back the window-curtain, looks out and says 'Once more my night's rest disturbed; no more sleep for me. Why must the Nazis always be so provocative and run about the place at night?' Gentleman, if everyone thought like that, then no one's sleep at night would be disturbed, it is true, but then the bourgeois today could not venture into the street. If everyone thought in that way, if these young folk had no ideal to move them and drive them forward, then certainly they would gladly be rid of these nocturnal nights . . . Believe me, there is already in all this the force of an ideal – a great ideal. And if the whole of Germany today had the same faith in its vocation as these hundred thousands, if the whole nation possessed this idealism, Germany would stand in the world otherwise than it stands now . . .

And so in contrast to our own official government I cannot see any hope for the resurrection of Germany if we regard the foreign politics of Germany as the primary factor; the primary necessity is the restoration of a sound German body politic armed to strike. In order to realise this ideal I founded thirteen years ago the National Socialist movement; that movement I have led during the last twelve years and I hope that one day it will accomplish this task and that, as the fairest result of its struggle, it will leave behind it a German body politic completely renewed internally, intolerant of anyone who sins against the nation and its interests, intolerant of anyone who will not acknowledge its vital interests or who opposes them, intolerant and pitiless against anyone who shall attempt once more to destroy or disintegrate this body politic. And yet ready for friendship and peace with anyone who has a wish for peace and friendship.

Source: Kaes, A., Jay, M., and Dimedberg, E. (eds), *The Weimar Republic Sourcebook*, Berkeley: University of California Press, 1994, pp. 138–141.

Document 17   EDGAR JUNG ON THE 'CONSERVATIVE REVOLUTION'

In this document, Edgar Jung, a leading Conservative journalist, describes the change in attitudes in Germany during 1932.

We currently find ourselves in the midst of a German revolution that can scarcely be expected to manifest itself in such forms as the French did through the storming of the Bastille. It will be protracted like the Reformation, but it will still leave its mark all the more fundamentally on the countenance of humanity. It will prompt a ruthless revision of all human values and dissolve all mechanical forms. It will oppose the driving intellectual forces, the formulas and the goals born of the French revolution. It will be the great conservative revolution that puts an end to occidental humanity, founding a new order, a new ethos and a new unity in the West under German leadership . . . The language of the German revolution will be . . . a world language. In the struggle for our self preservation we will, for the first time, speak a language that captures the hearts of other peoples . . . It is possible to maintain that it is necessary for National Socialism to be permeated by the spiritual renaissance with which Germany has been blessed in the last decade. Yet it is permissible to attribute a more limited historical task to National Socialism, the destruction of a rotten world and the preparation of the great field upon which the new seed is to be sown. This much is certain: the longing of all the masses making sacrifices today for National Socialism springs from the great conservative genetic inheritance that stirs within them and compels them to such action. Whether – to continue in the language of racial hygiene – the phenomenal form of this longing which goes today under the name of National Socialism, predominantly bears the traits of the conservative revolution or the liquidation of liberalism . . . The mighty energies that pulse through the German people are indestructible . . . That is why our hour has come: the hour of the German revolution.

Source: Jung, E., 'Deutschland and die Konservative Revolution' in *Deutsche uber Deutschland*, Munich: Albert Langen, 1932, pp. 369–382.

Document 18   'HOW DO WE STRUGGLE AGAINST A THIRD REICH?': THE VIEWS OF
A GERMAN NOVELIST

In this document, written in 1931, Lion Feuchtwänger, a popular novelist from the Weimar era, offers concerns about a Germany led by Adolf Hitler.

The war liberated the barbarian instincts of the individual and society to a degree that was previously unimaginable. National Socialism has skilfully organised the barbarity. Among the intellectuals it is called OBG: Organised Barbarity of Germany.

Anti-logical and anti-intellectual in its being and ideology, National Socialism strives to depose reason and install in its place emotion and drive – to be precise, barbarity. Just because intellect and art are transnational, National Socialism distrusts and hates them to the extreme. To gag the intellect and art is one of the most important parts of its programme and since it proclaims that they can be accomplished with the least danger, it is here that it has its greatest success.

As National Socialism has risen in influence, it has turned with a particular fanaticism against everything intellectual and everything artistic.

Nearly without a struggle the liberal bourgeoisie has cleared all cultural positions for its advance. Aside from a couple of workers' theatres, no cinema, nor theatre dares any longer to portray material hostile to the National Socialists . . . Not for a century has the mind in Germany been so unfree as it is today.

What the intellectuals and artists have therefore to expect once the Third Reich is definitely established is clear: extermination. And that is what the majority does expect. Those intellectuals who can do so are already preparing to emigrate. Anyone who moves among intellectuals in Berlin gets the impression that Berlin is a city full of future émigrés.

It is therefore the demand of naked self-preservation that all intellectuals struggle with body and soul and all their abilities against the Third Reich. As long as there remains a single corner in Germany where art is allowed to open its mouth, we want to pronounce it unmistakably and hammer it through the skull; the Third Reich means the extermination of science, of art, and of the intellect.

Source: Kaes, A., Jay, M., and Dimedberg, E. (eds.), *The Weimar Republic Sourcebook*, Berkeley: University of California Press, 1994, p. 167.

JOSEPH GOEBBELS INSTRUCTS PARTY WORKERS TO TONE DOWN   **Document 19**
'RADICAL' ASPECTS OF THE NAZI PROGRAMME

In the following document, Joseph Goebbels instructs party workers not to attack business.

In every political situation we must adhere to the old, tried guidelines of National Socialism, not treating all business alike in the Marxist way, but distinguishing strictly between healthy business leadership, which is indispensable to the economy and exploiters. To talk of expropriation of all industrial concerns is, of course, a direct contravention of National Socialist principles.

Source: Noakes, J., and Pridham, G., *Nazism 1919–1945. Vol. 1: The Rise to Power, 1919–1934*, Exeter: University of Exeter Press, 1983, pp. 107–108.

Document 20   COUNTDOWN TO HITLER COMING TO POWER

In the following document, Joachim von Ribbentrop, a young member of the Nazi Party, describes, in note-form, the negotiations which led to Hitler coming to power in January 1933.

Wednesday 18 January: Hitler insists on being Chancellor. Papen again considers this impossible. His influence with Hindenburg was not strong enough to effect this. Hitler makes no further arrangements for talks . . .

Sunday 22 January: Hitler talks alone to young Hindenburg for two hours, followed by Hitler-Papen talk. Papen will now press for Hitler as Chancellor, but tells Hitler that he will withdraw from these negotiations forthwith if Hitler has no confidence in him . . .

Monday 23 January: In the morning Papen saw Hindenburg, who refused everything . . .

Wednesday 25 January: Hitler's Chancellorship under the auspices of a national front does not appear quite hopeless. Young Hindenburg promises to talk to Joachim again before his father makes final decision . . .

Friday 27 January: Hitler back in Berlin. Long talk with him at Goring's flat . . . Hitler declares that he has said all he wants to say to the Field Marshal [Hindenburg] and does not know what to add. Joachim persuades Hitler that this last attempt should be made, and that the situation is by no means hopeless . . . I have never seen Hitler in such a state; I proposed to him and Goring that I should see Papen alone that evening and explain the whole situation to him. In the evening I saw Papen and convinced him eventually that the only thing that made sense was Hitler's Chancellorship and that he must do what he can to bring this about . . .

Saturday 28 January: About 11 a.m. I went to see Papen who received me with the question: 'Where is Hitler?' I told him that he had probably left, but could perhaps be contacted in Weimar. Papen said that he had to get back without delay: a turning point had been reached; after a long talk with Hindenburg, he, Papen, considered Hitler's Chancellorship possible . . .

Sunday 29 January: At 11 a.m. long Hitler-Papen talk. Hitler declared that on the whole everything was clear. But there would have to be general elections and an Enabling Law. Papen saw Hindenburg immediately. I lunched with Hitler at the Kaiserhof. We discussed the elections. As Hindenburg does not want these, Hitler asked me to tell the President that these would be the last elections. In the afternoon Goring and I went to Papen. Papen declared that all obstacles are removed and that Hindenburg expects Hitler tomorrow at 11 a.m. [to appoint him as Chancellor].

Monday 30 January: Hitler appointed Chancellor.

Source: Noakes, J., and Pridham, G., *Nazism 1919–1945. Vol. 1: The Rise to Power, 1919–1934*, Exeter: University of Exeter Press, 1983, pp. 118–120.

HITLER'S VIEWS ON ANTI-SEMITISM   **Document 21**

In 1919 Hitler wrote the following letter to a 'Herr Gemlich' who had sought his views on the 'Jewish Question'.

September 16, 1919

Dear Herr Gemlich,

The danger posed by Jewry for our people today finds expression in the undeniable aversion of wide sections of our people. The cause of this aversion is not to be found in a clear recognition of the consciously or unconsciously systematic and pernicious effect of the Jews as a totality upon our nation. Rather, it arises mostly from personal contact and from the personal impression which the individual Jew leaves almost always an unfavourable one. For this reason, antisemitism is too easily characterized as a mere emotional phenomenon. And yet this is incorrect. Antisemitism as a political movement may not and cannot be defined by emotional impulses, but by recognition of the facts. The facts are these: First, Jewry is absolutely a race and not a religious association. Even the Jews never designate themselves as Jewish Germans, Jewish Poles, or Jewish Americans but always as German, Polish, or American Jews. Jews have never yet adopted much more than the language of the foreign nations among whom they live. A German who is forced to make use of the French language in France, Italian in Italy, Chinese in China does not thereby become a Frenchman, Italian, or Chinaman. It's the same with the Jew who lives among us and is forced to make use of the German language. He does not thereby become a German. Neither does the Mosaic faith, so important for the survival of this race, settle the question of whether someone is a Jew or nonJew. There is scarcely a race whose members belong exclusively to just one definite religion.

Through thousands of years of the closest kind of inbreeding, Jews in general have maintained their race and their peculiarities far more distinctly than many of the peoples among whom they have lived. And thus comes the fact that their lives amongst us a non German, alien race which neither wishes nor is able to sacrifice its racial character or to deny its feeling, thinking, and striving. Nevertheless, it possesses all the political rights we do. If the ethos of the Jews is revealed in the purely material realm, it is even clearer in their thinking and striving. Their dance around the golden calf is becoming a merciless struggle for all those possessions we prize most highly on earth.

The value of the individual is no longer decided by his character or by the significance of his achievements for the totality but exclusively by the size of his fortune, by his money.

The loftiness of a nation is no longer to be measured by the sum of its moral and spiritual powers, but rather by the wealth of its material possessions.

This thinking and striving after money and power, and the feelings that go along with it, serve the purposes of the Jew who is unscrupulous in the choice of methods and pitiless in their employment. In autocratically ruled states he whines for the favour of 'His Majesty' and misuses it like a leech fastened upon the nations. In democracies he vies for the favour of the masses, cringes before the 'majesty of the people,' and recognises only the majesty of money.

He destroys the character of princes with byzantine flattery, national pride (the strength of a people), with ridicule and shameless breeding to depravity. His method of battle is that public opinion which is never expressed in the press but which is nonetheless managed and falsified by it. His power is the power of money, which multiplies in his hands effortlessly and endlessly through interest, and which forces peoples under the most dangerous of yokes. Its golden glitter, so attractive in the beginning, conceals the ultimately tragic consequences. Everything men strive after as a higher goal, be it religion, socialism, democracy, is to the Jew only means to an end, the way to satisfy his lust for gold and domination.

In his effects and consequences he is like a racial tuberculosis of the nations.

The deduction from all this is the following: an antisemitism based on purely emotional grounds will find its ultimate expression in the form of the pogrom. An antisemitism based on reason, however, must lead to systematic legal combating and elimination of the privileges of the Jews, that which distinguishes the Jews from the other aliens who live among us (an Aliens Law). The ultimate objective [of such legislation] must, however, be the irrevocable removal of the Jews in general. For both these ends a government of national strength, not of national weakness, is necessary.

The Republic in Germany owes its birth not to the uniform national will of our people but the sly exploitation of a series of circumstances which found general expression in a deep, universal dissatisfaction. These circumstances however were independent of the form of the state and are still operative today. Indeed, more so now than before. Thus, a great portion of our people recognizes that a changed state form cannot in itself change our situation. For that it will take a rebirth of the moral and spiritual powers of the nation.

And this rebirth cannot be initiated by a state leadership of irresponsible majorities, influenced by certain party dogmas, an irresponsible press, or internationalist phrases and slogans. [It requires] instead the ruthless installation of nationally minded leadership personalities with an inner sense of responsibility.

But these facts deny to the Republic the essential inner support of the nation's spiritual forces. And thus today's state leaders are compelled to seek support among those who draw the exclusive benefits of the new formation of German conditions, and who for this reason were the driving force behind the revolution the Jews. Even though (as various statements of the leading personalities reveal) today's leaders fully realized the danger of Jewry, they (seeking their own advantage) accepted the readily proffered support of the Jews and also returned the favour. And this payoff consisted not only in every possible favouring of Jewry, but above all in the hindrance of the struggle of the betrayed people against its defrauders, that is in the repression of the antisemitic movement.

Respectfully,

Adolf Hitler

Source: Eberhard Jäckel (ed.), *Hitler. Sämtliche Aufzeichnungen 1905–1924*, Stuttgart, 1980, pp. 88–90.

HITLER DEFINES THE DIFFERENCE BETWEEN THE NAZI PARTY AND THE **Document 22**
TRADITIONAL GERMAN CONSERVATIVE PARTY

In this document, written by Hitler in 1922, the Nazi leader outlines the nature of National Socialism and its position on the right of German politics.

Nothing is more liable to render the entire German-National (*deutsch-völkisch*) movement, if not actually barren from the outset, then yet ineffective in its results, than the total lack of understanding of the fact that every idea is without value so long as its aim is not translated into action, but remains forever thought alone.

And, in the same way, no danger that is motivated by deliberate evil can ever be conquered through the mere recognition of its harmful nature or motivating power, but only through the deliberate confrontation with another power. In the whole of Russia there may today remain no more than 600,000 persons among its 150 million who are not horrified by the Jewish dictatorship of blood and its satanic infamy. Nevertheless, millions of helpless people suffer under the 600,000 destroyers, because the conviction of the latter expresses itself in bloody terror, but among the millions it is no more than impotent wishing perhaps despite their better knowledge . . . .

And the German-National movement may well be the only one to realize that the whole internal structure of our state is not Germanic, but rather Semitic, that all our actions, even our thinking, are today no longer German but Jewish.

The movement may bewail a hundred times that our people are being destroyed by the poison of a monster that is so alien to its inner feeling; it may discern that class struggle and party disputes will rob us of the last remnant of resistance; it may foresee with prophetic spirit that we too shall sink into the blood-swamp of Bolshevism, and may prove a thousand times that the ultimate cause of all this misery, that the ultimate germ of this disease of the race is the Jew – the German-National movement may recognize this, but it will not be able to help and cannot do so, until it leaves the field of theoretical knowledge and replaces it with the decision to transform understanding into political power: to replace long-suffering scholarly study with the willingness to apply the organization of power . . . And yet this is the real cause of the disintegration of our people. This cursed splitting of the nation into two classes that today oppose each other as enemies to the death is our worst misfortune, and it alone is the reason why there is no hope for a better future for our nation.

For this reason only that movement which removes Germany's greatest national misfortune will be able to call itself National.

The movement which will no longer be proletarian and may no longer be bourgeois, but will be simply German.

The movement which unites those that strengthen this Germanism (*Deutschtum*) day by day, not only in words but in all the thousand fold deeds of human activity. . . .

In them lies the eternal fountain of the strength of our people. In them lies the future of our race. Whoever divides them strikes at Germany. Whoever unites them is National.

Finally, only that movement is national which does not bind this strength in order to lame it, but binds it in order to cast it as a solid block into the battle for victory for our own race.

And this battle will not be fought by majorities and parliamentary groups, but by the only form of majority that has shaped the fates of nations and states on this earth as long as it has existed. The majority of power and of the greater will and the strength to apply this power without consideration for mere numbers. To be German-National means not to dream today but to be a revolutionary; it means not to make do with academic knowledge; it means to have the passionate will to let deed some day follow on word.

Hundreds of thousands already know today what we need. But millions long for salvation. The first deed must today be to create an organization, from house to house, that will weld together the hundreds of thousands of the determined in order to fulfil the profound longings and hopes of the best of our people.

To liberate our race from inside, to free it from its chains on the outside. . . .

Source: Institute of Contemporary History (IfZ), Munich. Ausgewaehlte Dokumente zur Geschichte des nationalsozialismus ('Selected Documents in the History of National-Socialism').

MEETING OF HITLER AND HINDENBURG, 13 AUGUST 1932 **Document 23**

The following document is an affidavit, written by Otto von Meissner, chief of Presidential Chancellery, presented at Nuremberg Trial, 1946.

Hindenburg replied that because of the tense situation he could not in good conscience risk transferring the power of the government to a new party such as the National Socialists, which did not command a majority and which was noisy, intolerant and ill-disciplined. At this point, Hindenburg, with a certain show of excitement, referred to several recent occurrences – clashes between the Nazis and the police, acts of violence, committed by Hitler's followers against those who were of different opinion, excesses against Jews and other illegal acts. All these incidents had strengthened him in his conviction that there were numerous wild elements in the Party beyond control . . . After extended discussions Hindenburg proposed to Hitler that he declare himself ready to co-operate with other parties, in particular with the Right and Centre and he should give up the one-sided idea that he must have complete power. In co-operating with the other parties, Hindenburg declared, he would be able to show what he could achieve and improve upon. If he could show positive results, he would acquire immediately increasing and even dominant influence even in a coalition government. Hindenburg stated that this would be the best way to eliminate the widespread fear that a National Socialist government would make ill use of its power and would suppress all viewpoints and gradually eliminate them. Hindenburg states that he was ready to accept Hitler and the representatives of his movement in a coalition government, the precise combination to be a matter of negotiation, but that

he could not take the responsibility of giving exclusive power to Hitler alone
. . . Hitler was adamant, however, in refusing to put himself in a position of
bargaining with the leaders of the other parties and in such a manner to form
a coalition government.

Source: Bundesarchiv, Nuremberg Documents. 508/3309.

Document 24   THE APPEAL OF NATIONAL SOCIALISM TO YOUTH

*This is an extract from the Schenzinger's novel Hitlerjung, Quex (Hitler Youth
Quex); here the hero of the novel is walking in the forest when he spots a
Hitler Youth camp.*

The glow from the fire became brighter and brighter. The sound of the singing floated across to him again, quite clearly now. He could even hear a tune
that he had heard before, but could not remember when. It was a marching
song and it took hold of him. He ran up the hill and started to gaze at the
dazzling flames. He stood still and saw at least a thousand youths standing
around. Each held a pole with a flag that was brilliant red with a jagged
symbol. Each youth looked like everyone else with shorts, a brown shirt and
white handkerchief knotted around the neck. His heart was pounding. They
all looked towards the fire. A tall young man started speaking to them. He used
the words 'movement' and 'leader'. He moved closer and then 'Deutschland,
Deutschland uber alles' swept over him from a thousand voices like a wave.
I am a German too, he thought and he wanted to sing along with all the
others, but his voice failed him. This was German soil in a German forest and
he stood apart and he did not know what to make of it all except he felt a
great and sudden feeling of wanting to belong.

Lessing, H. and Liebel, M., *Wilde Cliquen*, Bensheim, 1981, p. 153.

References

Allen, W. (1995) *The Nazi Seizure of Power. The Experience of a Single German Town*, 2nd edn., London: Eyre and Spottiswoode.

Bullock, A. (1962) *Hitler. A Study in Tyranny*, London: Penguin.
Burleigh, M. (2000) *The Third Reich. A New History*, London: Pan.

Childers, T. (1983) *The Nazi Voter. The Social Foundations of Fascism in Germany, 1919–1933*, Chapel Hill: University of North Carolina Press.

Evans, R. (2003) *The Coming of the Third Reich*, London: Allen Lane.

Fest, J. (1974) *Hitler*, London: Weidenfeld & Nicolson.
Fischer, C. (1995) *The Rise of the Nazis*, Manchester: Manchester University Press.

Geary, R. (1993) *Hitler and Nazism*, London: Routledge.

Hitler, A. (1936) *Mein Kampf*, London: Paternoster.

Kater, M. (1993) *The Nazi Party. A Social Profile of Members and Leaders 1919–1945*, Oxford: Blackwell.
Kershaw, I. (2000) *The Nazi Dictatorship. Problems and Perspectives of Interpretation*, 4th edn., London: Edward Arnold.
Kershaw, I. (1998) *Hitler, 1889–1935, Hubris*, London: Allen Lane.
Kubizek, A. (1954) *Young Hitler*, London: Eyre and Spottiswoode.

Machtan, L. (2001) *The Hidden Hitler*, London: Perseus.
Mosse, G. (1966) *The Crisis of German Ideology. Intellectual Origins of the Third Reich*, London: Weidenfeld & Nicolson.
Muhlberger, D. (1991) *Hitler's Followers, Studies in the Sociology of the Nazi Movement*, London: Routledge.

Orlow, D. (1973) *The History of the Nazi Party, Vol. 1, 1919–1933*, Newton Abbot: David and Charles.

Payne, S. (1995) *A History of Fascism*, London: University College of London Press.

Shirer, W. (1961) *The Rise and Fall of the Third Reich*, London: Pan.

Toland, J. (1976) *Hitler*, London: Pan.

Waite, R. (1977) *The Psychopathic God. Adolf Hitler*, New York: Basic Books.

Zalampas, M. (1989) *Adolf Hitler and the Third Reich in American Magazines, 1923–1939*, Bowling Green, OH: Bowling Green State University Press.

Bibliographical essay

This very brief bibliographical essay is designed to provide the reader with some suggestions for further reading. The list is confined to books published in English.

For those who wish to study the subject in real depth, see Kehr, H. and Langmaid, J. (1980) *The Nazi Era, 1919–1945. A Selected Bibliography of Published Works from Early Roots to 1980*, London: Mansell.

There are a wide range of studies on the rise to power of Adolf Hitler and the Nazi Party. The most outstanding collection of original documents, with a very good commentary can be found in Noakes, J. and Pridham, G. (eds) (1983–1998), *Nazism. A Documentary Reader. Vol. 1: The Rise to Power, 1919–1934* (Exeter: Exeter University of Press), which contains some interesting documents from the years 1919 to 1933. For a useful examination of the historical debate surrounding all aspects of the rise and fall of the Third Reich, see Kershaw, I. (2000) *The Nazi Dictatorship. Problems and Perspectives of Interpretation*, 4th edn. (London: Edward Arnold). See also a superb collection of essays in Kershaw, I. (ed.) (1990) *Weimar. Why did German Democracy Fail?*, London: Weidenfeld & Nicolson.

There are many useful introductions to the subject, though most of these are focused on the Weimar Republic rather than specifically on the Nazi Party, most notably, Broszat, M. (1987) *Hitler and the Collapse of Weimar Germany* (Oxford: Berg); Burleigh, M. (2000) *The Third Reich. A New History*, London: Pan; Evans, R. (2003) *The Coming of the Third Reich*, London: Allen Lane; Eyck, E. (1967) *A History of the Weimar Republic, 2 vols.*, London: Wiley; Feuchtwanger, E. (1993) *From Weimar to Hitler*, London: Macmillan; Hiden, J. (1996) *The Weimar Republic*, 2nd edn., London: Longman; Kolb, E. (1988) *The Weimar Republic*, London: Unwin Hyman; Nicholls, A.J. (1992) *Weimar and The Rise of Hitler*, London: Macmillan; Peukert, D. (1991) *The Weimar Republic. The Crisis of Classical Modernity*, London: Allen Lane. All these studies attempt to explain the climate of politics in Weimar Germany and to weave the rise of the Nazis within a broader analytical framework.

For the impact of the Versailles settlement and the foreign policy debate in Germany during the Weimar era see: Adamthwaite, A. (1980) *The Lost Peace, 1918–1939. International Relations in Europe*, London: Edward Arnold; Henig, R. (1984) *Versailles and After*, London: Routledge; Hiden, J. (1993) *Germany and Europe 1918–1939*, 2nd edn., London: Longman; Jacobson, J. (1972) *Locarno Diplomacy*, Princeton: Princeton University Press.

For the economic problems of the Weimar era, the following studies may be read with profit: Evans, R. and Geary, D. (1987) *The German Unemployed, 1918–1936*, London: Croom Helm; Ferguson, N. (1995) *Paper and Iron. Hamburg Business and German Politics in the era of Inflation 1897–1927*, Cambridge: Cambridge University Press; Guttman, W. and Meehan, P. (1975) *The Great Inflation, 1923*, Farnborough: Saxon House; James, H. (1986), *The German Slump. Politics and Economics, 1924–1936*, Oxford: Oxford University Press; Overy, R. (1982) *The Nazi Economic Recovery*, London: Macmillan; Ringer, J. (1969) *The German Inflation of 1923*, Oxford: Oxford University Press; Stachura, P. (ed.) (1987), *Unemployment and the Great Depression in Weimar Germany*, London: Macmillan; Turner, H. (1985) *German Big Business and the Rise of Hitler*, Oxford: Oxford University Press.

For the role of the army in the politics of the Weimar era see: Carsten, F. (1966), *The Reichswehr and Politics, 1918–1933*, Oxford: Oxford University Press; Gordon, H. (1957), *The Reichswehr and the German Republic, 1919–1926*, Princeton: Princeton University Press; Wheeler-Bennet, J. (1961) *Nemesis of Power. The German Army in Politics, 1918–1945*, London: Macmillan. For the various paramilitary groups that operated within Germany see: Diehl, J. (1977) *Paramilitary Politics in Weimar Germany*, Bloomington: Indiana State University Press.

For information on the political parties in Weimar, the following studies are useful: Breitman, R. (1981) *German Socialism and Weimar Democracy*, Chapel Hill: University of North Carolina Press; Evans, E. (1981) *The German Centre Party 1870–1933*, Illinois: Illinois University Press; Fischer, C. (1991) *The German Communists and the Rise of Nazism*, London: Macmillan; Guttsmann, W. (1981) *The German Social Democratic Party 1875–1933*, London: Allen and Unwin; Hertzmann, L. (1963) *DNVP – Right-wing Opposition in the Weimar Republic*, Lincoln: Nebraska University Press; Jones, L. (1993) *Between Reform and Resistance. Studies in the History of German Conservatism from 1789 to 1945*, Oxford: Berg.

For the role played by President Hindenburg in the downfall of the Weimar Republic, examine: Dorpalen, A. (1964), *Hindenburg and the Weimar Republic*, Princeton: Princeton University Press; Wheeler-Bennet, J. (1936) *Hindenburg. The Wooden Titan*, London: Macmillan. For the role of Heinrich Brüning see Patch, W. (1998) *Heinrich Brüning and the Dissolution of the Weimar Republic*, Cambridge: Cambridge University Press.

There are also many useful studies, which concentrate on the internal history of the Nazi Party before 1933, most notably, Fischer, C. (1995) *The Rise of the Nazis*, Manchester: Manchester University Press, which not only provides some excellent insights into the supporters of Nazism, but also contains some good original documents. See also: Orlow, D. (1973) *The History of the Nazi Party, Vol. 1, 1919–1933*, Newton Abbot: David and Charles, which remains the standard work on the inner workings of the Nazi Party before 1933. For Nazi youth activism see: Stachura, P. (1975) *Nazi Youth in the Weimar Republic*, London: Clio Press.

For three useful micro studies of the Nazi Party at the local level, before 1933, see: Allen, W. (1966) *The Nazi Seizure of Power. The Experience of a Single German Town, 1930–1935*, London: Eyre and Spottiswoode; Noakes, J. (1971) *The Nazi Party in Lower Saxony, 1921–1933*, Oxford: Oxford University Press; Pridham, G. (1973) *Hitler's Rise to Power. The Nazi Movement in Bavaria, 1923–1933*, London: Hart-Davis. The most exhaustive study of the membership of the Nazi Party remains: Kater, M. (1993) *The Nazi Party. A Social Profile of Members and Leaders 1919–1945*, Oxford: Blackwell. A recent study which takes issue with Kater's view of middle-class over-representation in the membership of the Nazi Party is: Muhlberger, D. (1991) *Hitler's Followers. Studies in the Sociology of the Nazi Movement*, London: Routledge.

The two most useful studies of Nazi electoral support before 1933 are Childers, T. (1983) *The Nazi Voter. The Social Foundations of Fascism in Germany, 1919–1933*, Chapel Hill: University of North Carolina Press, and Hamilton, R. (1982) *Who Voted For Hitler?* Princeton: Princeton University Press. See also: Childers, T. (ed.) (1986) *The Foundations of the Nazi Constituency, 1919–1933*, London: Croom Helm. The most impressive German language study of Nazi voting patterns, based on a sophisticated computer analysis is Falter, J. (1991) *Hitlers Wahler*, Munich: C.H. Beck.

Among the hundreds of biographies of Adolf Hitler, the best and most up to date is the two-volume life by Ian Kershaw. Volume 1 deals with Hitler's rise to power. See Kershaw, I. (1998) *Hitler, 1889–1936, Hubris*, London: Allen Lane. The most famous is: Bullock, A. (1962) *Hitler. A Study in Tyranny*, London: Penguin, which now seems dated as it downgrades the importance of ideology and views Hitler as merely a power-crazed opportunist. A much more penetrating and original analysis of Hitler's early life, and the rise to power of the Nazi Party can be found in Fest, J. (1974) *Hitler*, London: Weidenfield & Nicolson, which examines the German archives in detail and provides some excellent psychological insights into the Nazi dictator. See also, Maser, W. (1973) *Hitler*, London: Allen Lane; Toland, J. (1976) *Adolf Hitler*, New York: Doubleday, and Stone, N. (1980) *Hitler*, London: Hodder and Stoughton. For a psychological analysis of Hitler's life see: Waite, R. (1977) *The Psychopathic God. Adolf Hitler*, New York: Basic Books.

For Nazi ideology see: Geary, R. (1993) *Hitler and Nazism*, London: Routledge, which provides some very penetrating insights; Lane, B. and Rupp, L. (eds) (1978) *Nazi Ideology before 1933*, Manchester: Manchester University Press; Payne, S. (1995), *A History of Fascism*, London: University College of London Press; Mosse, G. (1966) *The Crisis of German Ideology. Intellectual Origins of the Third Reich*, London: Weidenfeld & Nicolson.

Index